Act One

Edited by David Self and Ray Speakman

Stanley ～～～～～ **ers) Ltd**

Originally published in 1979 by Hutchinson Education

Reprinted in 1989 by
Stanley Thornes (Publishers) Ltd
Ellenborough House
Wellington Street
CHELTENHAM GL50 1YW

98   99   00   /   20   19   18   17   16

British Library Cataloguing in Publication Data

Act 1
  1. Radio plays   2. Television plays
  I. Self, David   II. Speakman, Ray
  822'.02   PN6120.R2

  ISBN 0 7487 0183 4

Set in IBM Press Roman

Printed and bound in Great Britain at Redwood Books, Trowbridge.

Contents

Introduction

Of the four plays published for the first time in this collection, *Our Day Out* was written for television and the other three for radio.

The first of these radio plays was commissioned from the Liverpool playwright Alan Bleasdale by BBC School Radio. It takes its title from a popular song, and looks at the ways in which people (and especially young people) see 'young love'. It is about two teenagers, Mickey and Dawn, who are set a project by their English teacher in which they have to work as a pair, like two reporters, to find out what 'young love' means to a number of people. But Mickey has intended to spend the evening watching his team, Liverpool, play at home; also, he has little intention of co-operating with a 'mere' girl. However, in the hope that Dawn will write up their project while he goes to the match, he agrees to accompany her on a number of 'interviews'. They visit Dawn's grandfather, her older married sister and her mother, and from their conversations with these people we hear what 'young love' means to people of different generations. Dawn eventually talks Mickey into taking her to the match with him, and by the end of the play Mickey's attitudes have changed somewhat — though he has certainly not become the complete romantic by any means.

Indeed Mickey remains cynical throughout the play — possibly because (like many boys of his age) he feels in some way inferior or inadequate compared with the more mature and more confident

Dawn; and his cynicism is a way of compensating. However, despite this, he remains affable and good-tempered – even when Dawn goads him so that she will get her own way.

Though it is set in the 'public' world of the classroom and football match, it is a very private play – being, as it is, about true love between young people. The author is very aware of their attitudes and preoccupations and he draws his characters with sensitivity and care, but he is also aware of their wit and humour. The result is an admirably 'un-soppy', funny and realistic play which will strike many a chord in classrooms where there is some kind of tacit war or hostility between boys and girls. It will also evoke many memories among older readers.

Love is a Many Splendoured Thing is essentially a play about the relationships between two people. So, too (but in a very different mood), is *On the Face of It.*

Set in an old man's garden, it is about a fourteen-year old boy, Derry, whose face has been badly disfigured in an accident. He climbs into the garden, and when he comes face to face with the old man, Mr Lamb, he expects him to be put off by the sight of his face (as most people are). But Mr Lamb is different: he engages Derry in conversation about a variety of things.

Derry is at first bitter and suspicious, thinking Mr Lamb is only changing the conversation. Gradually though, as the old man reveals that he too is handicapped (he has lost a leg), and as he asks Derry a number of unexpected questions, Derry begins to relax and even to admit that he enjoys being with Mr Lamb. He remains somewhat cautious, but Mr Lamb has sown in him a new confidence and enthusiasm for living, and Derry volunteers to help the old man to pick up his crab apples. First, though (because it is getting late), he must go home to tell his mother where he is. Predictably she is suspicious of the eccentric old man and tells Derry to stay at home, but Derry knows that he must return: 'If I don't go back there, I'll never go anywhere in this world again.' So he runs back to the garden, only to find that Mr Lamb has got the ladder out, begun picking the apples, fallen and died.

In this play, Susan Hill has written powerfully and simply about a most moving situation. Derry is isolated by his disfigurement – cut off from others and, justifiably, bitter about his fate. Mr Lamb is similarly isolated, an eccentric and solitary old man. But from Mr Lamb, Derry learns the importance of having a positive attitude to life, and at the same time develops confidence and independence, both of which he realizes will be necessary to him in the future. At the tragic climax of the play, we are left to ponder whether what Derry has learned will be undone by the accident of the old man's death.

Though the play is about an extreme physical disfigurement, it says much about those who feel isolated for other reasons, and suggests what they might achieve if they can only summon up the courage to come out of what might be a self-imposed prison. It also poses many questions about the ways we regard and treat such people.

The central character in *Mr Bruin Who Once Drove the Bus* is also something of a misfit, but Don Haworth's treatment of the theme is light-hearted. That is not to say his play is without its serious moments, and even a touch of near-tragic pathos.

Kindly Mr Bruin drives a bus which, every day, makes a circuit of a number of villages, picking up schoolchildren and taking them to school in the nearby town. So kind is Mr Bruin that he goes out of his way to give lifts to those who need them and waits for those who are late. The result is that the bus is always late getting to school, the pupils arriving each morning during a different line of the hymn being sung in assembly.

Under pressure from a local councillor, the Director of Education and parents, the Headmaster tells Mr Bruin to drive faster and keep better time. His subsequent speeding only causes more complaints, but his final undoing comes when (out of a readiness to do someone a favour) he dresses up as an elephant as part of an advertising stunt at the local supermarket. After the resulting chaos, he is deemed 'irresponsible', but with typical good nature he takes it upon himself to resign his position and to move on to another post.

Of the three radio plays in this collection, *Mr Bruin Who Once Drove the Bus* is the one which makes fullest use of radio techniques. Frequently the humour comes from the way speeches are delivered, or from sound effects and music. For this reason, it is a play that will repay being rehearsed and worked on before being 'presented' in any way. It is a rich anthology of comic eccentrics — Mr Bruin himself, the pompous Councillor Garbage, the would-be reasonable Headmaster and the doubly afflicted Mr Pilchard (whose speeches will certainly require rehearsal before being read or spoken aloud). It is also a play which says much about the way society expects us to conform to established patterns and to accept narrow confines of authority. Primarily, though, it is a fine piece of comedy writing — but it is also much more.

So too is *Our Day Out,* but because this is a highly amusing play, we should not forget that it poses a number of serious questions and, in particular, ones about authority, discipline and freedom in school.

Like Alan Bleasdale, Willy Russell writes about the people of his home city, Liverpool. His play chronicles a school outing: the Progress Class (i.e. a class for those with reading and writing problems) in an inner-city Liverpool school is being taken by coach on a day trip to Conway in North Wales. In charge of the outing is the class teacher, the easy-going and motherly Mrs Kay — who, incidentally, is nobody's fool. However, fearing what may result from her tolerant attitudes, the Headmaster sends the very much stricter Mr Briggs along as well 'just to try and keep things in some sort of order'. Much of the play is taken up with the different reactions of these two teachers to the behaviour of the pupils at a roadside café, a zoo, at Conway Castle itself and later on the beach.

Woven into what Briggs sees as a running battle between himself and Mrs Kay are a number of other story lines — for example, the relations between two younger teachers and the older boys and girls, and the problems of Carol, the girl to whom life offers so little in inner Liverpool that she is prepared not to go back. It is her threatened suicide that produces the climax of the day and almost brings about a change in Briggs's attitudes.

How Briggs will behave the day after the outing is just one of the many questions posed by Willy Russell's play, questions which will stimulate much discussion. Few of his characters are drawn in terms of black and white or good and evil. The moment one finds oneself 'siding' with a particular character or group of characters, they 'let you down', and the final reaction is that, while the play is frequently very funny, it is also an ultimately saddening picture of life as it is.

The realism of the play (as well as its humorous way of posing serious problems) was perhaps what caused it to be so well received when first shown on television. The *Daily Express* described it as a 'stunner', and 'a trip that shouldn't be missed': it is no wonder then that within six weeks of its first transmission it was repeated on BBC 1 as 'Play for Today'.

Effective and challenging though it will be in the classroom, it cannot be forgotten that it was written for television. Furthermore, although it is convenient to describe it as a play, it was not written as a play to be recorded in a television studio but as a film to be made on location. For this reason, special thought must be given as to how best the script can be read in a particular classroom or presented for an audience. Indeed discussion of how best the script can be 'lifted off the page' in particular local circumstances can be a valuable and creative activity in English and drama lessons, as also (it is hoped) will be the suggestions for follow-up work included at the end of the book.

Notes on Presentation

Reading

Even the most informal classroom reading of a playscript is
helped by rehearsal. Remember, not even the experienced
professional actor is happy to sight-read, but usually prefers to
have had the chance at least to look over his part before a first
reading in front of his colleagues. So, once a play has been cast,
those who will be reading should be given the chance to look over
their lines, make sure they know where they enter and exit, when
to pause and when to 'come in quickly' at the end of the previous
speech, and indeed that they appreciate the mood, etc., of their
character at any given moment.

Note that (especially in the case of those plays with small
casts) it is possible for a class to break up into small groups, and
for each group to rehearse its own interpretation of the play,
before one group presents its reading to the whole class.

Note too that it is much easier to read to a class from the front
of a traditional classroom, and from a standing position or a
position where you can be seen by your 'audience'.

In preparing the scripts for inclusion in this book, we have
re-written the technical directions in the radio plays and the
author's 'visual' directions in the filmscript; these directions (i.e.
the ones printed between speeches), along with the scene titles,
may be read aloud by an 'announcer'. In a classroom presentation,
it might be helpful if the announcer were in view of the 'audience'
but away from the acting area.

Tape-recording

The most obvious and natural way of presenting the three radio scripts is, of course, to record them on tape. When this is done, then the directions will be translated back into sound effects or realized by the actors' movements, etc.

The following points may be of help:

a   Discover the directional qualities of your microphone – that is, from how wide an angle it picks up sound.

b   Even the best microphone cannot produce a good recording over a long distance from the sound source. For speech, it should be 30 – 40 cm from the mouth. (Those readers with stronger voices can obviously be further away than those who do not project so well.)

c   It is much easier to record a play with the actors standing rather than sitting. (They can then easily tiptoe away when not involved in a dialogue, and so allow those who are speaking to stand in the best positions.)

d   Don't hold the script between mouth and microphone, and avoid rustling pages.

e   Rooms with bare walls are unsuitable for making recordings in, as they have a very echo-y sound. Where possible, use a carpeted, curtained room (unless of course an echo-y effect is required!).

f   It is possible to minimize echo (and also to lessen background noise) by speaking closer to the microphone and by turning down the recording level. When doing this, a better sound may be achieved by speaking across the microphone rather than directly into it.

g   Sound effects are important in creating a sense of location. Either they can be 'spot effects' created at the time of recording (e.g. doors opening and closing, cups of tea being poured, etc.) or recorded (either on another tape or from commercial discs). Don't worry about including every sound – concentrate on background noises which suggest location (e.g. traffic noises, bus interiors, etc.) and those sounds which indicate the arrival or departure of a character. Don't allow clumsy and accidentally comic sounds (like artificial footsteps) to clutter or confuse the much more important dialogue.

h Gently fading out the very last few words or sounds of a scene and fading in the first sounds of a new scene will suggest a transition from one scene to another.

Staging

A distinguishing feature of radio and television plays (and for that matter, of films) is that, unlike stage plays, they can make speedy transitions from one scene to another; and they can also include scenes which actually involve travel (e.g. scenes where characters walk along a street or travel by bus).

When presenting plays like these on stage (whether it be in a formal production or informally to just a small audience) thought must be given as to how they can be adapted and still maintain their necessary pace.

On the Face of It (because it almost all takes place in one location) can be fairly easily adapted for a stage performance. Obviously the directions must be converted into stage directions (and perhaps added to), which the cast can act out. (NB It might be worth discussing whether it would be more dramatic for Derry to recall his conversation with his mother as a soliloquy rather than staging it as a short separate scene; and whether it might also be more effective for the audience not to see Mr Lamb's fall, but to 'discover' his accident, with Derry.)

The other plays will require less realistic and more symbolic production. The use of specially taken 35mm slides or projected scenery will be a useful way of announcing location to an audience, and the use of sound effects (especially in such scenes as those inside the buses in *Mr Bruin Who Once Drove the Bus* and in *Our Day Out*, at the football match in *Love is a Many Splendoured Thing*, and in the outdoor scenes in *Our Day Out* can be a highly effective substitute for scenery.

In order to preserve fluency and speed of staging, the use of stage furniture should be restricted — it can only get in the way of the action.

Note that Mickey, at the beginning of *Love is a Many Splendoured Thing,* and the pupil who acts as narrator in *Mr Bruin Who Once Drove the Bus* are kinds of *compère* characters who speak directly to the audience. They should not speak 'cold' between action, but rather 'commentate' on mimed action as it happens. It would be possible to write in a similar part for another member of the Progress Class, who would act as commentator or story-teller in *Our Day Out.* Care should be taken, though, that such a character does not hold up the action. Alternatively, of course, such narration could be acted out in a traditional way.

Acknowledgements

For permission to publish the plays in this volume, the editors are grateful to the following authors and their agents:

Alan Bleasdale and Harvey Unna & Stephen Durbridge Ltd for *Love is a Many Splendoured Thing*; Susan Hill and Richard Scott Simon Ltd for *On the Face of It;* Don Haworth and Harvey Unna & Stephen Durbridge Ltd for *Mr Bruin Who Once Drove the Bus* and Willy Russell and Margaret Ramsay Ltd for *Our Day Out.*

No performance of these plays may be given unless a licence has been obtained. Applications should be addressed to the authors or their agents.

Love is a Many Splendoured Thing

Alan Bleasdale

Characters

Mickey Murray
Dawn Darnell
Mr Pitt (their English teacher)
Dawn's Grandad
Janet (Dawn's older married sister)
Mrs Darnell (Dawn's mother)
Other class members
Football crowd

First broadcast on BBC School Radio, 3 March 1978

Love Is a Many Splendoured Thing

Scene: **A classroom** [*The song* – Love is a Many Splendoured Thing – *plays by way of introduction. As the music fades, the sounds of a classroom can be heard. A lesson is going on.* **Mickey** *speaks directly to the audience*]

Mickey: Do you like songs and poetry? Do you? You'd like our English lessons then. I'm not kidding, we've got this English teacher, Mr Pitt, who thinks that there's nothing else in life but poems. Honest. He's the kind of bloke who'd like to see 'Coronation Street' done in rhyming couplets. Whatever it is we're doing, he drags poetry into it. Take this morning's lesson. We began this project on 'young love', didn't we? Well, I needn't tell you he was in his element, wasn't he? And do y'know what the first thing was that he did? He made us sit next to a girl. A girl! Urgh! That's about as bad as having a whole week of needlework lessons. And do you know who he made me sit next to? Dawn Darnell. Now, some of the others in the class might fancy that, 'cos she's supposed to be good-looking, but I'll tell you this now f'free — one big rope hanging around your neck, that's all a girl is. Once you're holding hands and going for walks in the park, you might as well kiss the world good-bye, 'cos your happy days are over and gone.

[*Towards the end of* **Mickey's** *introduction,* **Mr Pitt's** *voice can be heard reading an extract from* Twelfth Night]

Mickey: Listen, he's at it now. Mr Pitt, 'Cess' for short, the Poet
Laureate of St Patrick's Comprehensive. . . .

Mr Pitt: 'What is love? 'tis not hereafter;
Present mirth hath present laughter;
What's to come is still unsure:
In delay there lies no plenty;
Then come kiss me, sweet and twenty,
Youth's a stuff will not endure.'

[*The* **Class** *fidgets. coughs and desk-moving can be heard*]

Mr Pitt: Right, now then, Four Alpha, can any of you tell me
something about that?

Mickey: Yes sir, me sir.

Mr Pitt: Go on then, Murray.

Mickey: It was another poem.

[*There are a few sniggers*]

Mickey: It was, it rhymed: 'plenty' and 'twenty'.

Mr Pitt: [*Without malice*] And in your case, Murray, it could
so easily be 'empty'.

Mickey: I am a bit hungry, sir.

Mr Pitt: [*Sighs*] You're incorrigible, aren't you, Murray?

Mickey: No, sir, I'm a Catholic.

[*Laughter from the rest of the* **Class**]

Mr Pitt: All right, all right. Anybody else? Yes, Dawn?

Dawn: Sir, the poem's about young love, and the poet's saying
that you should enjoy it while it's here, because we don't know
what the future holds for us, and one thing's certain, we won't
be young for ever.

Mr Pitt: Very good, Dawn. . . .

Mickey: [*Whisper*] Know it all. Teacher's pet. [*Makes sucking noises*] Creep, creep. . . .

Dawn: Oh, go away. . . .

Mr Pitt: And this afternoon we have also studied what 'young love' means — not just to the young, but to different generations. . . .

[*The bell goes and the* **Class** *immediately begins to shuffle.* **Mr Pitt** *calls out above the noise*]

Mr Pitt: Er, just hang on a moment, now for the homework tonight. . . .

[*The* **Class** *half-heartedly moans and mumbles*]

Mr Pitt: . . . for the homework tonight, I want you to keep in the groupings you're in now, one boy and one girl, and I want you to work as a couple, like two reporters. . . .

[**Mickey** *groans*]

Dawn: [*To* **Mickey**] It's worse for me — I've got to work with you.

Mickey: Very funny. Anyway, I'm going to the match tonight. Liverpool're at home.

Mr Pitt: Murray, may I remind you of what happens in this school if homework isn't done on time?

Mickey: Oh, sir, but. . . .

Mr Pitt: No 'buts', Murray. Detention. And I'm equally sure you need no reminding that *tomorrow* night the fourth-year football team have a very important. . .

Mickey: [*Muttering*] I get the picture. . . .

Mr Pitt: Now, all of you, I want you to talk to the people you know, your parents, your brothers and sisters, and I want you to find out what 'young love' means to them. Not what it used to mean once, but what it means *now*. Tomorrow we'll all present our findings. Okay, off you go, next lesson. . . .

[*The* Class *departs*]

Mickey:　Can't we find out on our own, sir?

Mr Pitt:　No, Murray. That's one of the purposes of the exercise. I'm fed up with this class split right down the middle, with the boys on one side and the girls on the other.

Mickey:　But I live miles and miles away from Dawn Darnell, sir. By the time I got to her house, it'd be time for me to go home again.

Mr Pitt:　Do I look soft, Murray?

Mickey:　[*Pause*] No, sir.

Mr Pitt:　So it won't surprise you to know that I took the precaution of checking your addresses before the lesson, Murray. You're sitting next to Dawn because she happens to be the girl who lives nearest to you.

Mickey:　[*Lying*] We moved house yesterday, sir.

Mr Pitt:　Go on, get to your next lesson, and grow up.

Scene:　**A street**　[*In the background the noise of traffic and pedestrians can be heard as* Dawn *and* Mickey *talk*]

Mickey:　Look, Dawn, tell you what, you write yours and I'll write mine, and tomorrow morning we'll compare. What do you say?

Dawn:　No.

Mickey:　Great what do you mean 'no'?

Dawn:　I think Mr Pitt's right. The lads in our class act like babies. It's about time you lot realized we're human beings as well. And it's about time you grew up.

Mickey: Oh no, not you and all. He said that.

Dawn: Well, it's true. Girls grow up quicker than boys.

Mickey: Rubbish.

Dawn: It's not.

Mickey: Prove it.

Dawn: Well, for a start, most girls in our class prefer talking to lads who are older than them — and that's because the boys their age are still messing about with train sets and push bikes. Even you, Mickey, you might think you're smart because you're the captain of the football team and you're the cross-country champion. . . .

Mickey: For the county. . . .

Dawn: But you're still a kid. No one in their right mind would fall in love with you.

Mickey: Great. Suits me fine. But I'm no kid, Dawn, an' don't you go calling me one, or else. . . .

Dawn: Or else what? You'll sulk? Run home to mummy?

Mickey: Get lost! [*Pause*] Ah, come on, Dawn, be a sport, don't be sly.

Dawn: See, you're acting like a baby now.

Mickey: Right, you asked for it. I'll go around with you, I'll stand there while you ask all these soppy questions, I'll miss the match, but don't expect me to change, don't expect me to turn around and be David Essex or Robert Redford. I'm me, I'm Mickey Brown, I'm nearly fifteen, I like football, fishing, basketball and running; and I don't like girls. An' what's more, you're not coming to our house.

Dawn: Do you practise making speeches? Do you stand in front of the mirror and rehearse?

Mickey: Oh, come on, let's get it over with. Where're we going first?

Dawn: My grandad's flat's just around the corner. . . .

Scene: **Dawn's grandad's flat** [Grandad *is pouring tea*]

Grandad: How many sugars, young man?

Mickey: Two please, Mr Darnell. . . . See you support Liverpool, then? That's some collection of programmes.

Grandad: A lifetime's hobby, lad. Now then. . . .

Dawn: We want to ask you some questions, Grandad.

Grandad: What is this – 'Mastermind'?

Dawn: No, really, we just want to know what you think . . . how you feel . . . [*Beginning to feel ill at ease*] . . . about, well, young love.

Grandad: [*Laughs*] It's too young for me.

Mickey: [*Quietly*] An' me.

Grandad: Ah, but there was a time, there was that . . . what!

Dawn: So you didn't think it was soft when you were younger?

Grandad: Oh well, when I was Mickey's age, I had better things to do. . . . [*Laughs*]

Mickey: See, Dawn.

Grandad: . . . that is, I thought I did. If you'd have told me when I was fourteen that I'd be courting strong at seventeen, I could have laughed in your face. And to think I was married a year later. . . .

Mickey: At eighteen?

Grandad: First World War, lad: 1917, heading for the trenches in France. Most who went there never came back . . . a lot of us who went got married beforehand . . . you know. . . .

Dawn: Undying love?

Grandad: Aye. Thought we might never see each other again. Three days before I was called up, we got married. Our honeymoon was a weekend in North Wales. I can remember it as if it were yesterday. First night we got there, we decided we wanted to go somewhere sort of romantic and, you know, exchange rings. Well, we walked up this lane heading for the top of a hill; the first snow of winter at the very top . . . an' when we got up there, we stood together, me and your grandmother, holding hands, looking down at the lights in the houses in the valley. The moon was shining on the sea, and the stars were in the sky, and I gave her my ring and she gave me hers, like we had done in church, and we stood there for ages, thinking the whole world was ours, till in the end the moon went behind the clouds and it got too cold to stand. And then I took two paces down the hill in the dark and fell over a dead sheep.

Mickey: [*Laughing loudly*] That's brilliant.

Grandad: Yes, even then it was funny.

Mickey: I'm going to use that in the project. Liven the lesson up a bit tomorrow.

Dawn: But what about *today*, Grandad? What do you think about young people falling in love now?

Grandad: Things are different now, aren't they? More freedom for your generation, more money, more time an' all. I worked twelve-hour shifts for nowt more than a couple of bob.

Dawn: Do you think that's a good thing, Grandad? You know, all the freedom that courting couples have today. All the discos and the clubs, staying out later, not having to be chaperoned if you go out with someone. It seems much easier than before from what I've been told.

Grandad: You're right, it is. It's easier to fall in love, and easier to fall out of love as well. When things are easy, you sometimes don't value them as much as you should. That's my only complaint, Dawn. That, and the fact that I'm not young today. By God, I wish I was.

Mickey: But y'know, a lot of old people — well, not even the really old ones like. . . .

Grandad: Like me, you mean?

Mickey: I'm sorry, I wasn't being funny or anything. . . .

Grandad: Go on lad, it's all right.

Mickey: Well, even our parents, they go on about how lucky we are, and how ungrateful we are, and if only we knew what they had to put up with. They make you feel guilty just to be young.

Grandad: And you know why that is, Mick? Because they're jealous, a lot of them: not just jealous of what you've got, but jealous because of what you are. You're young, and they're not. [*Pause, then deliberately cheerful*] Right then, has that answered your questions?

Dawn: Yes thanks, Grandad.

Mickey: I've got one more question for you.

Grandad: Fire away then.

Mickey: Are you going to the match tonight?

Grandad: [*Laughing*] I wish I was.

Scene: **The street**   [**Dawn** *and* **Mickey** *talk above the traffic noise.*]

Mickey: He's great, your grandad, isn't he? I mean, you can talk to him, like.

Dawn: I thought you would get on with him.

Mickey: Well, he supports the right team, doesn't he? Okay, where next?

Dawn: My married sister, Janet. That is, she used to be
married.

Scene: **Dawn's sister's house**   [Janet *answers* Dawn's *question.*]

Janet: [*Rapid*] Young love? You want to know about young
love? I'll tell you about young love, I'll tell you about all kinds
of love. *It's all lies,* from beginning to end.

Dawn: But Janet. . . .

Janet: You don't know, Dawn, you're too young. When I was
your age I was starry-eyed as well. I believed in true love and
romance and knights in shining armour and the sugar candy
mountains. And as far as I'm concerned, they're all fairy stories.
[*Pause for breath*]

Mickey: Er, y'know, if I'm in the way, I'd be happy to. . . .

Janet: I don't mind.

Mickey: As a matter of fact, I'm not really interested in, er,
young love . . . or any sort of . . . anything like that.

Janet: Well, take a tip from me, stay that way.

Dawn: Right . . . er, that was. . . .

Janet: Short and sour?

Dawn: Something like that.

Janet: You shouldn't have asked me. You know how I feel. I'm
not going to be once bitten, twice bitten.

Dawn: That's why we did ask you. We wanted as many opinions
as possible. Anyway, we'll be going. . . . I'll come over tomorrow.

Scene: **On the street again**

Mickey: Your Janet certainly made herself clear.

Dawn: Yeah. . . . She never used to be like that. When I was in the infants she was forever starry-eyed about someone or other, going around the house singing "All you need is love". . . .

Mickey: And all I need is me tea. See y'.

Dawn: Where are you going?

Mickey: Home for my tea. I'm starving.

Dawn: Come to ours.

Mickey: Me?

Dawn: Don't worry, Mickey, it's dark, no one'll see you.

Mickey: Do you have chips?

Dawn: [*Laughs*] Most nights. Come on, we can ask my Mum what she thinks.

Mickey: About chips?

Dawn: Young love!

Mickey: Oh *that*!

Scene: **Dawn's house**   [**Mickey** *and* **Dawn** *eat as her mother,* **Mrs Darnell**, *pours tea.*]

Dawn: [*With some impatience*] Look, Mum, I know you and Dad have always been happy, but I'm sure Mickey doesn't want to have the history of our family presented to him. . . .

Mrs Darnell: You liked looking at those photos, didn't you, Mickey?

Mickey: [*Slight pause*] Great, just great. I liked the one with Dawn wearing a brace on her teeth and pigtails. . . .

Dawn: Don't start, Mickey. . . .

Mickey: And the one where you'd just been sick on the sands at Southport. Good, that, Dawn. . . .

Dawn: Look, Mum, I told you. . . .

Mrs Darnell: There's some cake in the back kitchen, Dawn.

Mickey: Cake as well?

Dawn: [*Going off*] You're a right guzzler, you are, Mickey Murray. You want to see him at school dinners, Mum. The other lads call him the dustbin, cos he'll take anything.

[**Dawn** *leaves the room, closing the door behind her*]

Mickey: [*Calling after her*] I don't. I always leave my semolina. And pilchards.

Mrs Darnell: What is it you want to know, Mickey?

Mickey: Me? I don't want to know anything. Your Dawn's the leader of this expedition. I'm just along for the ride.

Dawn: [*From outside*] Young love, Mum. We want to know what you think about it.

Mrs Darnell: Oh, it's wonderful. The memories I've got of when I was young, when I met Dawn's father. . . . . There's one time when we first met. . . .

[**Dawn** *opens the door*]

Dawn: [*Coming in*] Mother! You've started again. I can't go into class tomorrow and tell Mr Pitt all about your courting days. It's not History, it's English.

Mrs Darnell: And don't be so cheeky, madam. All I was going to say was that some couples are happy when they're young, and they stay happy together as they get older. For them, young love works out. For others, it doesn't.

Mickey: [*Quietly*] I know.

Mrs Darnell: You met our Janet, didn't you?

Mickey: Yes. [*Pause*] It's like, well, we've got a photo of my Mam and Dad at home from years ago. And you want to see them, they're laughing fit to bust, linking arms . . . and . . . just happy. . . .

Mrs Darnell: When you've been married for a long time, you don't have to jump and shout and laugh a lot to be happy together, Mickey. That's for when you're young.

Mickey: How do you know if young love's going to turn out to be . . . I dunno . . . old love – or any love at all? It's like playing the pinball machine. It's just chance most of the time.

Mrs Darnell: Ah now, there, I think you're wrong, Mick. When a boy and a girl first start going out together, it might seem silly and soft, and have something to do with chance, but suddenly for the first time two young people share things. They share their time together, they share their thoughts, their hopes, their dreams, and if they're mature enough, they care for each other. And they wouldn't be in love if they weren't attracted to each other. Now does that sound like a pinball machine?

Dawn: That's just what I think as well, Mum.

Mickey: Ah, but you're, y'know, women. You're different.

Mrs Darnell: It's all the same, for all of us. As the poet said, 'If music be the food of love, dance on.' That should interest you.

Mickey: I don't like dancing neither.

Mrs Darnell: I meant the food.

Dawn: [*Poetically*] 'Love makes the world go around.'

Mickey: You two sound just like Mr Pitt. Why couldn't he give us proper homework, like 'A day in the life of a penny', or 'What I did on my holidays', or something. Young love. It's nearly enough to put me off that cake. But, er, not quite.

[**Mrs Darnell** *laughs*]

Scene: **Later, at the Darnell's front door**

Mickey: No, listen, honest, it was a lovely tea, er, no, y'don't have to see me to the gate, Dawn, I'll be back in a bit, cross my heart, I'll just slip home, tell my Mam where I am, and then, quick as a flash. . . .

Dawn: [*Smiling*] Liar!

Mickey: What?

Dawn: Liar.

Mickey: Oh. Er, I thought you said that. But it's never crossed my mind to sneak off to the match, really it hasn't, and I'm not in a hurry 'cos it's only forty-five minutes to kick off, or anything like that. . . . No, listen, I can walk home on my own. . . .

Dawn: I'll just go to the newsagent's by your house. I've got a magazine to pick up.

Mickey: And then I suppose you'll walk back to ours with me, just for the company, and then. . . .

Dawn: Walk all the way home again. With you.

Mickey: Look, let's get one thing straight, I'm only doing this so I can play football tomorrow night. It's no fun for me, you know, walkin' around playing reporters for the last three hours. I've interviewed your grandad, your sister, your mother, seen the family album and had a smart meal, but that's enough. I can write it all up when I get back from the . . . er, taking the dog for a walk.

Dawn: Fair enough, Mick. I've been mean to you. We'll come to an arrangement.

Mickey: Okay, I'll go to the match and you write it up. Great, thanks, Dawn. See y'.

Dawn: No, we both watch the football and we both write it up.

Mickey: Suits me, but who're you going to the game with?

Dawn: You.

Mickey: Me?

Dawn: You.

Mickey: I'm not taking a girl to a football match. Sorry.

Dawn: Why not?

Mickey: Er . . . it's not allowed. There's a law against it.

Dawn: How strange. I usually go with my dad and *we've* never been stopped.

Mickey: You go to the match?

Dawn: Every home game. I'd be going tonight except my dad's working.

Mickey: [*Genuinely amazed*] Gerraway, I never knew that.

Dawn: How could you? We've been in the same class for four years and never spoke, except to insult each other.

Mickey: I remember lending you a dinner ticket once in the second year.

Dawn: Only because it was pilchards and semolina.

Mickey: [*Laughs*] I bet it was an' all. [*Pause*] Do you really want to come with me?

Dawn: Yes.

Mickey: We'll go the Anfield Road end then.

Dawn: Is that where you usually go?

Mickey: No chance. I go on the Kop, but I'm not letting my mates see me with a girl.

Dawn: [*Laughing*] I might have known . . . hang on, I'll just get my magazine. . . .

Scene: **At the match**   [*Before the kick off. There is a general hubbub from the crowd rather than hysteria.* **Mickey** *and* **Dawn**

are reading from a magazine, although the audience should realize this only gradually]

Dawn: '. . . But I have always secretly loved you, darling.'

Mickey: [*Quieter, more reluctant*] 'And I have also loved you, dearest, but was afraid of showing my true feelings.'

Dawn: 'You were my first love.'

Mickey: 'Young love.'

Dawn: 'True love! Oh Michael. . . .'

Mickey: Shush! Steady on, they'll all hear us. That bloke with the rosette's already moved up three steps for a listen.

Dawn: That's not what it says in the magazine.

Mickey: Yeah, I know. It says, 'Penelope, please marry me and be mine forever', but if you're expecting me to shout that out in a crowd of fifty thousand, you've had it. And that magazine of yours is soft. People don't go around saying things like that.

Dawn: Penelope and Michael are a bit wet, aren't they.

Mickey: You're not kiddin'. Look at them — look at the picture. Since when has everyone been blonde, blue-eyed, good-looking, dressed to kill, no pimples and a sports car? With the guarantee of a happy ending.

Dawn: People like a happy ending. Don't they? Don't you?

Mickey: [*Pause*] Yeah. About ten past nine tonight.

[*The crowd roars*]

Mickey: Here they are!

Scene: **After the match** [**Dawn** *and* **Mickey** *walk along the street with the crowd leaving the football ground. There is a lot of noise and laughter. The home team has won*]

Mickey: . . . and that third goal, Dawn, did you see that? The way he climbed up to beat the centre half . . . sheer class.

Dawn: And their goal was a mile offside.

Mickey: Doesn't matter. Four-one. Glad we went, aren't you? Hey, you know when we were arguing about doing this project and whether I was going to the match or not, did you . . . did you have it sort of planned then that I'd take you?

Dawn: [*Mock innocence*] The thought never entered my head!

Mickey: Do y'know what – you're almost as sly as me! [*Laughs*] Anyway, here we are, your road. You don't really want me to help you write it out, do you? You're much better than me at that sort of stuff.

Dawn: So long as we can get together for a few minutes before the lesson. But there is one big gap in the whole project.

Mickey: What?

Dawn: Well, we've got an example of what an old person thinks about young love, what someone who's out of love thinks of it, and what one middle-aged parent thinks; but we haven't heard from anyone who's actually in the middle of it all.

Mickey: You mean. . . .

Dawn: That's right, young and in love.

Mickey: You can make that up.

Dawn: But we really should ask someone.

Mickey: Who? Imagine me going up to one of my mates and saying, 'Er, excuse me, Macker, but do you happen to be in love at the present moment, and could you give me a few words about what it's like. . . .'

Dawn: Why don't you ask me?

Mickey: What do you know abou– . . . who're you in love with?

Dawn: Someone who probably isn't really worth loving. . . .

Mickey: I bet it's that Jimmy Swift out of the fifth form. Just 'cos he's got a motorbike.

Dawn: No, it's not.

Mickey: Well, what's it like then?

Dawn: [*Giggles*] It's silly and soft and sloppy and sort of stupid. . . .

Mickey: Sounds about right. . . .

Dawn: . . . but it's also all the things the magazines say. You see him and you really do go all funny inside, you can't help watching him and seeing his better qualities, and forgetting that, well, that he's a bit big-headed, rude and awkward and bad-mannered and too good at football and cross country for his own good. . . .

Mickey: Dawn, listen. . . .

Dawn: . . . and when you hear people talking about him behind his back, you don't join in any more, and then before long you want to talk to him, be with him, have a. . . .

Mickey: If this is a joke. . . .

Dawn: Have a good time with him. Nothing serious, no moon-lighting or eloping. . . .

Mickey: [*Going off*] Er, yeah, great. Just remembered, must dash. . . . [*He starts to run*]

Dawn: [*Calling*] Mickey. . . .

Mickey: [*Distant*] Ta – ra!

Scene: **The classroom**

Dawn: . . . and so, in conclusion, sir, we found that young love means all kinds of things to all kinds of different people. Everyone has a different viewpoint, mainly as a result of what has happened to them; there are no clear-cut rules and regulations like there are for other things in life, like driving a car or playing football or attending school. [*Pause*] That's it, sir.

Mr Pitt: Very good indeed. Some excellent research and thought there, Dawn. I presume that these are your conclusions as well, Murray?

Mickey: [*Jokingly*] Er . . . what? Oh aye, I agree with Dawn, sir. [*Serious, to himself*] Every word.

Mr Pitt: [*Distant*] I must say, before we move on to the next couple and their findings, that what you say does remind me of John Donne's immortal lines in 'Love's Progress', when he says:
'Whoever loves, if he do not propose
The right true end of love, he's the one that goes
To sea for nothing but to make him sick. . . .'

[*As* **Mr Pitt** *speaks,* **Dawn** *whispers across to* **Mickey**]

Dawn: Sorry about last night.

Mickey: So am I.

Dawn: You didn't do anything.

Mickey: Yes I did. I ran away. I never knew you fancied me.

Dawn: Shhhhh!

Mr Pitt: . . . and, of course, following on from that we have Shakespeare's lines: 'So true a fool is love that in your will/ Though you do anything she thinks no ill. . . .'

[**Dawn** *blows a raspberry*]

Mr Pitt: Murray, was that you?

[*The classroom noises fade as we hear the music to the song –* Love is a Many Splendoured Thing]

The End

On the Face of It

Susan Hill

Characters

Mr Lamb (in his seventies; elderly but not senile)
Derry (a boy aged 14)
Derry's Mother

First broadcast on BBC School Radio, 15 January, 1975

On the Face of It

Scene: **Mr Lamb's garden** [*There is the occasional sound of birdsong and of tree leaves rustling.* **Derry's** *footsteps are heard as he walks slowly and tentatively through the long grass. He pauses, then walks on again. He comes round a screen of bushes, so that when* **Mr Lamb** *speaks to him he is close at hand and* **Derry** *is startled*]

Mr Lamb: Mind the apples.

Derry: What? Who's that? Who's there?

Mr Lamb: Lamb's my name. Mind the apples. Crab apples those are. Windfalls in the long grass. You could trip.

Derry: I ... there ... I thought this was an empty place. I didn't know there was anybody here....

Mr Lamb: That's all right. I'm here. What you afraid of, boy? That's all right.

Derry: I thought it was empty ... an empty house.

Mr Lamb: So it is. Since I'm out here in the garden. It is empty. Until I go back inside. In the meantime, I'm out here and likely to stop. A day like this. Beautiful day. Not a day to be indoors.

Derry: [*Panic*] I've got to go.

Mr Lamb: Not on my account. *I* don't mind who comes into the garden. The gate's always open. Only *you* climbed the garden wall.

Derry: [*Angry*] You were watching me.

Mr Lamb: I saw you. But the gate's open. All welcome. You're welcome. I sit here. I like sitting.

Derry: I'd not come to steal anything.

Mr Lamb: No, no. The young lads steal . . . scrump the apples. You're not so young.

Derry: I just . . . wanted to come in. Into the garden.

Mr Lamb: So you did. Here we are, then.

Derry: You don't know who I am.

Mr Lamb: A boy. Thirteen or so.

Derry: Fourteen. [*Pause*] But I've got to go now. Good-bye.

Mr Lamb: Nothing to be afraid of. Just a garden. Just me.

Derry: But I'm not . . . *I'm* not afraid. [*Pause*] People are afraid of *me*.

Mr Lamb: Why should that be?

Derry: Everyone is. It doesn't matter who they are, or what they say, or how they look. How they *pretend*. I know. I can see.

Mr Lamb: See what?

Derry: What they think.

Mr Lamb: What do they think, then?

Derry: *You* think . . . 'Here's a boy.' You look at me . . . and then you see my face and you think, 'That's bad. That's a terrible thing. That's the ugliest thing I ever saw.' You think, '*poor* boy.' But I'm not. Not poor. Underneath, you're afraid. Anybody would be. I am. When I look in the mirror, and see it, I'm afraid of me.

Mr Lamb: No. Not of the whole of you. Not of *you*.

Derry: Yes!

[*Pause*]

Mr Lamb: Later on, when it's a bit cooler, I'll get the ladder and a stick, and pull down those crab apples. They're ripe for it. I make jelly. It's a good time of year, September. Look at them . . . orange and golden. That's magic fruit, I often say. But it's best picked and made into jelly. You could give me a hand.

Derry: What have you changed the subject for? People always do that. Why don't you ask me? Why do you do what they all do and pretend it isn't true and isn't there? In case I see you looking and mind and get upset? I'll tell . . . you don't ask me because you're *afraid* to.

Mr Lamb: You want me to ask . . . say so, then.

Derry: I don't like being with people. Any people.

Mr Lamb: I should say . . . to look at it . . . I should say, you got burned in a fire.

Derry: Not in a fire. I got acid all down that side of my face and it burned it all away. It ate my face up. It ate me up. And now it's like this and it won't ever be any different.

Mr Lamb: No.

Derry: Aren't you interested?

Mr Lamb: You're a boy who came into the garden. Plenty do. I'm interested in anybody. Anything. There's nothing God made that doesn't interest me. Look over there . . . over beside the far wall. What can you see?

Derry: Rubbish.

Mr Lamb: Rubbish? Look, boy, *look* . . . what do you see?

Derry: Just . . . grass and stuff. Weeds.

Mr Lamb: Some call them weeds. If you like, then . . . a weed garden, that. There's fruit and there are flowers, and trees and herbs. All sorts. But over there . . . weeds. I grow weeds there.

Why is one green, growing plant called a weed and another 'flower'? Where's the difference. It's all life . . . growing. Same as you and me.

Derry: We're not the same.

Mr Lamb: I'm old. You're young. You've got a burned face, I've got a tin leg. Not important. You're standing there . . . I'm sitting here. Where's the difference?

Derry: Why have you got a tin leg?

Mr Lamb: Real one got blown off, years back. Lamey-Lamb, some kids say. Haven't you heard them? You will. Lamey-Lamb. It fits. Doesn't trouble me.

Derry: But you can put on trousers and cover it up and no one sees, they don't have to notice and stare.

Mr Lamb: Some do. Some don't. They get tired of it, in the end. There's plenty of other things to stare at.

Derry: Like my face.

Mr Lamb: Like crab apples or the weeds or a spider climbing up a silken ladder, or my tall sun-flowers.

Derry: *Things.*

Mr Lamb: It's all relative. Beauty and the beast.

Derry: What's that supposed to mean?

Mr Lamb: You tell me.

Derry: You needn't think they haven't all told me that fairy story before. 'It's not what you look like, it's what you are inside. Handsome is as handsome goes. Beauty loved the monstrous beast for himself and when she kissed him he changed into a handsome prince.' Only he wouldn't, he'd have stayed a monstrous beast. I won't change.

Mr Lamb: In that way? No, you won't.

Derry: And no one'll kiss me, ever. Only my mother, and she kisses me on the other side of my face, and I don't like my mother to kiss me, she does it because she has to. Why should I like that? I don't care if nobody ever kisses me.

Mr Lamb: Ah, but do you care if *you* never kiss *them.*

Derry: What?

Mr Lamb: Girls. Pretty girls. Long hair and large eyes. People you love.

Derry: Who'd let me? No one.

Mr Lamb: Who can tell?

Derry: I won't ever look different. When I'm as old as you, I'll look the same. I'll still only have half a face.

Mr Lamb: So you will. But the world won't. The world's got a whole face, and the world's there to be looked at.

Derry: Do you think this is the world? This old garden?

Mr Lamb: When I'm here. Not the only one. But the world, as much as anywhere.

Derry: Does your leg hurt you?

Mr Lamb: Tin doesn't hurt, boy!

Derry: When it came off, did it?

Mr Lamb: Certainly.

Derry: And now? I mean, where the tin stops, at the top?

Mr Lamb: Now and then. In wet weather. It doesn't signify.

Derry: Oh, that's something else they all say. 'Look at all those people who are in pain and brave and never cry and never complain and don't feel sorry for themselves.'

Mr Lamb: I haven't said it.

Derry: 'And think of all those people worse off than you. Think, you might have been blinded, or born deaf, or have to live in a wheelchair, or be daft in your head and dribble.'

Mr Lamb: And that's all true, and you know it.

Derry: It won't make my face change. Do you know, one day, a woman went by me in the street – I was at a bus-stop – and she was with another woman, and she looked at me, and she said . . . whispered . . . only I heard her . . . she said, 'Look at that, that's a terrible thing. That's a face only a mother could love.'

Mr Lamb: So you believe everything you hear, then?

Derry: It was *cruel*.

Mr Lamb: Maybe not meant as such. Just something said between them.

Derry: Only I heard it. I heard.

Mr Lamb: And is that the only thing you ever heard anyone say, in your life?

Derry: Oh no! I've heard a *lot* of things.

Mr Lamb: So now you keep your ears shut.

Derry: You're . . . peculiar. You say peculiar things. You ask questions I don't understand.

Mr Lamb: I like to talk. Have company. You don't have to answer questions. You don't have to stop here at all. The gate's open.

Derry: Yes, but. . . .

Mr Lamb: I've a hive of bees behind those trees over there. Some hear bees and they say, bees *buzz*. But when you listen to bees for a long while, they humm . . . and hum means 'sing'. I hear them singing, my bees.

Derry: But . . . I like it here. I came in because I liked it . . . when I looked over the wall.

Mr Lamb: If you'd seen me, you'd not have come in.

Derry: No.

Mr Lamb: No.

Derry: It'd have been trespassing.

Mr Lamb: Ah. That's not why.

Derry: I don't like being near people. When they stare . . . when I see them being afraid of me.

Mr Lamb: You could lock yourself up in a room and never leave it. There was a man who did that. He was afraid, you see. Of everything. Everything in this world. A bus might run him over, or a man might breathe deadly germs onto him, or a donkey might kick him to death, or lightning might strike him down, or he might love a girl and the girl would leave him, and he might slip on a banana skin and fall and people who saw him would laugh their heads off. So he went into this room, and locked the door, and got into his bed, and stayed there.

Derry: For ever?

Mr Lamb: For a while.

Derry: Then what?

Mr Lamb: A picture fell off the wall onto his head and killed him.

[**Derry** *laughs a lot*]

Mr Lamb: You see?

Derry: But . . . you still say peculiar things.

Mr Lamb: Peculiar to some.

Derry: What do you do all day?

Mr Lamb: Sit in the sun. Read books. Ah, you thought it was an empty house, but inside, it's full. Books and other things. Full.

Derry: But there aren't any curtains at the windows.

Mr Lamb: I'm not fond of curtains. Shutting things out, shutting things in. I like the light and the darkness, and the windows open, to hear the wind.

Derry: Yes. I like that. When it's raining, I like to hear it on the roof.

Mr Lamb: So you're not lost, are you? Not altogether? You do hear things. You listen.

Derry: They talk about me. Downstairs. When I'm not there. 'What'll he ever do? What's going to happen to him when we've gone? How ever will he get on in this world? Looking like that? With that on his face?' That's what they say.

Mr Lamb: Lord, boy, you've got two arms, two legs and eyes and ears, you've got a tongue and a brain. You'll get on the way you want, like all the rest. And if you chose, and set your mind to it, you could get on *better* than all the rest.

Derry: How?

Mr Lamb: Same way as I do.

Derry: Do you have any friends?

Mr Lamb: Hundreds.

Derry: But you live by yourself in that house. It's a big house, too.

Mr Lamb: Friends everywhere. People come in . . . everybody knows me. The gate's always open. They come and sit here. And in front of the fire in winter. Kids come for the apples and pears. And for toffee. I make toffee with honey. Anybody comes. So have you.

Derry: But I'm not a friend.

Mr Lamb: Certainly you are. So far as I'm concerned. What have you done to make me think you're not?

Derry: You don't know me. You don't know where I come from or even what my name is.

Mr Lamb: Why should that signify? Do I have to write all your particulars down and put them in a filing box, before you can be a friend?

Derry: I suppose . . . not. No.

Mr Lamb: You could tell me your name. If you chose. And not, if you didn't.

Derry: Derry. Only it's Derek . . . but I hate that. Derry. If I'm your friend, you don't have to be mine. *I* choose that.

Mr Lamb: Certainly.

Derry: I might never come here again, you might never see me again and then I couldn't still be a friend.

Mr Lamb: Why not?

Derry: How could I? You pass people in the street and you might even speak to them, but you never see them again. It doesn't mean they're friends.

Mr Lamb: Doesn't mean they're enemies, either, does it?

Derry: No. They're just . . . nothing. People. That's all.

Mr Lamb: People are never just nothing. Never.

Derry: There are some people I hate.

Mr Lamb: That'd do you more harm than any bottle of acid. Acid only burns your face.

Derry: *Only. . . .*

Mr Lamb: Like a bomb only blew up my leg. There's worse things can happen. You can burn yourself away inside.

Derry: After I'd come home, one person said, 'He'd have been better off stopping in there. In the hospital. He'd be better off with others like himself.' She thinks blind people only ought to be with other blind people and idiot boys with idiot boys.

Mr Lamb: And people with no legs altogether?

Derry: That's right.

Mr Lamb: What kind of a world would that be?

Derry: At least there'd be nobody to stare at you because you weren't like them.

Mr Lamb: So you think you're just the same as all the other people with burned faces? Just by what you look like? Ah . . . everything's different. Everything's the same, but everything is different. Itself.

Derry: How do you make all that out?

Mr Lamb: Watching. Listening. Thinking.

Derry: I'd like a place like this. A garden. I'd like a house with no curtains.

Mr Lamb: The gate's always open.

Derry: But this isn't mine.

Mr Lamb: Everything's yours if you want it. What's mine is anybody's.

Derry: So I could come here again? Even if you were out . . . I could come here.

Mr Lamb: Certainly. You might find others here, of course.

Derry: Oh. . . .

Mr Lamb: Well, that needn't stop you, you needn't mind.

Derry: It'd stop *them*. They'd mind me. When they saw me here. They'd look at my face and run.

Mr Lamb: They might. They might not. You'd have to take the risk. So would they.

Derry: No, you would. You might have me and lose all your other friends, because nobody wants to stay near me if they can help it.

Mr Lamb: I've not moved.

Derry: No. . . .

Mr Lamb: When I go down the street, the kids shout 'Lamey-Lamb'. But they still come into the garden, into my house; it's a game. They're not afraid of me. Why should they be? Because I'm not afraid of them, that's why not.

Derry: Did you get your leg blown off in the war?

Mr Lamb: Certainly.

Derry: How will you climb on a ladder and get the crab apples down, then?

Mr Lamb: Oh, there's a lot of things I've learned to do, and plenty of time for it. Years. I take it steady.

Derry: If you fell and broke your neck, you could lie on the grass and die. If you were on your own.

Mr Lamb: I could.

Derry: You said I could help you.

Mr Lamb: If you want to.

Derry: But my mother'll want to know where I am. It's three miles home, across the fields. I'm fourteen, but they still want to know where I am.

Mr Lamb: People worry.

Derry: People fuss.

Mr Lamb: Go back and tell them.

Derry: It's three miles.

Mr Lamb: It's a fine evening. You've got legs.

Derry: Once I got home, they'd never let me come back.

Mr Lamb: Once you got home, you'd never let yourself come back.

Derry: You don't know . . . you don't know *what* I could do.

Mr Lamb: No. Only you know that.

Derry: If I chose. . . .

Mr Lamb: Ah . . . if you *chose*. I don't know everything, boy. I can't tell you what to do.

Derry: They tell me.

Mr Lamb: Do you have to agree?

Derry:　I don't *know* what I want. I want . . . something no one else has got or ever will have. Something just mine. Like this garden. I don't know what it is.

Mr Lamb:　You could find out?

Derry:　How?

Mr Lamb:　Waiting. Watching. Listening. Sitting here or going there. I'll have to see to the bees.

Derry:　Those other people who come here . . . do they talk to you? Ask you things?

Mr Lamb:　Some do, some don't. I ask them. I like to learn.

Derry:　I don't believe in them. I don't think anybody ever comes. You're here all by yourself and miserable and no one would know if you were alive or dead and nobody cares.

Mr Lamb:　You think what you please.

Derry:　All right then, tell me some of their names.

Mr Lamb:　What are names? Tom, Dick or Harry.
　　　[*Getting up*] I'm off down to the bees.

Derry:　I think you're daft . . . crazy. . . .

Mr Lamb:　That's a good excuse.

Derry:　What for? You don't talk sense.

Mr Lamb:　Good excuse not to come back. And you've got a burned-up face, and that's other people's excuse.

Derry:　You're like the others, you like to say things like that. If you don't feel sorry for my face, you're frightened of it, and if you're not frightened, you think I'm ugly as a devil. I *am* a devil. Don't you? [*Shouts*] Don't you?

[**Mr Lamb** *does not reply. He has gone to his bees*]

Derry:　[*Quietly*] No. You don't. I like it here.

[*Pause.* **Derry** *gets up and shouts*]

I'm going. But I'll come back. You see. You wait. I can run. I haven't got a tin leg. I'll be back. . . .

[**Derry** *runs off. Silence. The sound of the garden again*]

Mr Lamb: [*To himself*] There my dears. That's you seen to. Ah . . . you know. We all know. 'I'll come back.' They never do, though. Not them. Never do come back.

[*The garden noises fade*]

Scene: **Derry's house**

Mother: You think I don't know about him, you think I haven't heard things?

Derry: You shouldn't believe all you hear.

Mother: Been told. *Warned.* We've not lived here three months, but I know what there is to know and you're not to go back there.

Derry: What are you afraid of? What do you think he is? An old man with a tin leg and he lives in a huge house without curtains and has a garden. And I want to be there, and sit and . . . listen to things. Listen and look.

Mother: Listen to what?

Derry: Bees singing. Him talking.

Mother: And what's he got to say to you?

Derry: Things that matter. Things nobody else has ever said. Things I want to think about.

Mother: Then you stay here and do your thinking. You're best off here.

Derry: I hate it here.

Mother: You can't help the things you say. I forgive you. It's
bound to make you feel bad things . . . and say them. I don't
blame you.

Derry: It's got nothing to *do* with my face and what I look like.
I don't care about that and it isn't important. It's what I think
and feel and what I want to see and find out and hear. And
I'm going back there. Only to help him with the crab apples.
Only to look at things and listen. But I'm going.

Mother: You'll stop here.

Derry: Oh no, oh no. Because if I don't go back there, I'll
never go anywhere in this world again.

[*The door slams.* **Derry** *runs, panting*]

And I want the world . . . I want it. . . . I want it. . . .

[*The sound of his panting fades*]

Scene: **Mr Lamb's garden**   [*Garden sounds: the noise of a
branch shifting; apples thumping down; the branch shifting again*]

Mr Lamb: Steady . . . that's . . . got it. That's *it*. . . .

[*More apples fall*]

And again. That's it . . . and. . . .

[*A creak. A crash. The ladder falls back,* **Mr Lamb** *with it. A
thump. The branch swishes back. Creaks. Then silence.* **Derry**
opens the garden gate, still panting]

Derry: You see, you see! I came back. You said I wouldn't and
they said . . . but I came back, I wanted. . . .

[*He stops dead. Silence*]

Mr Lamb? Mr. . . . You've. . . .

[*He runs through the grass. Stops. Kneels*]

Mr Lamb? It's all right. . . . You fell. . . . I'm here, Mr Lamb. It's all right.

[*Silence*]

I came back. Lamey-Lamb. I did . . . come back.

[*Derry begins to weep*]

The End

Mr Bruin Who Once Drove the Bus

Don Haworth

Characters

Narrator
Mr Bruin, driver of a school bus
Headmaster
Boy
Girl
Woman
Fatty Foggon
Mr Pilchard
Councillor Garbage
Man
Other pupils, men and women

First broadcast on BBC School Radio, 7 February, 1975

Mr Bruin Who Once Drove the Bus

Scene: **The school hall**

Pupils: [*Singing to the piano*]
'Praise for the sweetness
Of the wet garden
Sprung in completeness
Where his feet pass.'
[*During the last two lines of the hymn a small hubbub is heard*]

Headmaster: [*Speaks*] Just a moment, Miss Winkle, please.
[*Calls*] The students just arrived from Mr Bruin's bus, don't attempt to push through to your usual places. Move along the wall and stay there. Quickly, please.

[*A buzz of movement*]

Mr Bruin, could we speak later? All right, Miss Winkle, proceed.

Pupils: [*Singing to piano*]
'Mine is the sunlight
Mine is the morning
Born of one light
Eden saw play.'

Scene: **The Headmaster's study**

Headmaster: Mr Bruin, Bill, please do understand, punctuality is essential.

Bruin: Yes, Headmaster. This poor old chap at Bench Road Ends. . .

Headmaster: Mr Bruin, your bus is a school bus. Poor old chaps by definition do not qualify.

Bruin: . . . has a mile to walk to his sister's. . . .

Headmaster: But it is against the regulations, Mr Bruin, to give lifts.

Bruin: His right leg, there's a gyrating movement at the hip followed by an outward thrust of the knee and kick of the toe. . . .

Headmaster: A disablement. I understand.

Bruin: As though his leg was operated on an eccentric cam.

Headmaster: Mr Bruin, I don't insist on the letter of the regulations. I turn a blind eye. But please, Bill, please, strive to arrive more punctually.

Bruin: Yes, Headmaster.

Headmaster: [*Brightly*] Make it your ambition.

Bruin: I will, Ernest.

Headmaster: [*With galloping enthusiasm*] Make it your aim, your target, your goal.

Bruin: Yes, Ernest.

Headmaster: So that one day we shall have the pleasure of chiselling on your headstone: 'Mr Bruin, as ever on time.'

[*The* **Headmaster** *laughs a ringing laugh;* **Mr Bruin** *gives an amused chuckle*]

Narrator: Mr Bruin drove us all in from the countryside. He was a big man with a jolly red face and a heavy moustache. His real name was Broom or something like that but one day just after he got the job a little girl called him Mr Bruin and it stuck. From behind he looked just like a bear sitting over his wheel with an old brown gingery coat stretched across his wide shoulders and his cap many sizes too small perched on his head. None of us knew what he had been or where he had come from but he was quite unlike anybody who had driven the bus before.

Scene: **Inside the bus**

Bruin: Good morning. This is your driver speaking. The outside temperature is 17 degrees Centigrade, pressure 1031 millibars. Our speed is 30 miles an hour and our estimated time of arrival 0850 hours.

Boy: Mr Bruin, can I record you on my cassette?

Bruin: On your what?

Boy: My cassette. In real aeroplanes. . . .

Bruin: Isn't this a real aeroplane?

Boy: But them that fly. Well, when it says this is your pilot speaking, well it isn't your pilot speaking.

Bruin: Then that's a lie.

Boy: No, it's a cassette.

Girl: A recording.

Bruin: Oh. Well, you do whatever's necessary, Albert.

Girl: Switch on. Go on, Mr Bruin. 'The farm we are passing to starboard. . . .'

Bruin: . . . is the property of Herbert Snout Esquire whose

comely daughter, Julie [**Boys** *shout*] is stepping up into the
Land-Rover [**Boys** *whistle*] whilst to port the good yeoman
himself is driving his three tractors along the skyline in toil so
ill-rewarded that he's hard put to it to find enough biscuit
tins. . . .

All children: [*Join him in shouting*] . . . to keep all his losses
in.

[*Everybody laughs*]

Girl: Mr Bruin, there's Mr Pickles holding up his stick again.

[*The bus brakes*]

Scene: **The school hall**   [*The piano can be heard accompanying the hymn*]

Pupils: [*Singing to piano, with echo*]
'God's recreation
Of the new day.'

Scene: **The Headmaster's study**

Headmaster: 'God's recreation', Mr Bruin.

Bruin: Yes, Headmaster.

Headmaster: 'Fresh from the word' is unacceptably late, 'Where
his feet pass' inexcusably so, but 'God's recreation', Mr Bruin,
it has the most frightful ring about it of being late not by
minutes but by millennia. [*Laughs ringingly*]

Bruin: You see, Headmaster, this old chap with the leg. . . .

Headmaster: Yes, mounted on an eccentric cam.

Bruin: . . . in deference to your wishes for prompt arrival made such haste down his garden path that his boot shot off and we were some time searching for it in the nettles.

Headmaster: Mr Bruin, the other drivers manage to arrive on time.

Narrator: Well they did and everybody knew why. If you weren't at the road end right on the dot they simply sailed past and some, seeing a boy or girl belting along a farm track, would deliberately step on it, leaving people stranded within yards of a pick-up point and on wet or slushy mornings half-drowning them with spray from the wheels.

Woman: Dear Headmaster Nothing in this missive should be took as reflecting on Mr Bruin's bus far from it it's a real pleasure for them all whipping along to school whereas at one time you'd have thought they was off to Borstal and the patience of that man he is kindness embodied sitting smoking his pipe while late scholars tumble out of bed and we have had some with Charlie because his dad who is thick overwound the alarm clock and bust the spring so we are among the worst culprits and I will not throw stones by mentioning other names though Fatty Foggon is one but however what with one and another of them it is seldom the bus arrives on time which brings me to my point which is it says in Charlie's report he has gaps in his knowledge well he might well have because of all this arriving late it's all right if your child is bright but Charlie's father is thick as mentioned above also his two brothers I think it is hereditary and three thick uns in one house is quite enough to wreck you without Charlie going that way so would you please top up the gaps in his knowledge which the lad is not to blame for and oblige yours respectfully Connie Cupboard.

Headmaster: [*Dictating*] Dear Mrs Cupboard: Thank you for your letter of the 23rd – and I think if you would, Miss James, just the usual: points noted and will be very much borne in mind. Now the Director of Education's note on the same theme, what are we to reply? [*Pause*] Informal. A clean breast. My dear Charles: I am sorry our old friend Councillor Garbage is snapping at your heels again. Full stop. What he says is true. Full stop. The bus driven by the new driver has arrived sometimes less punctually than we would have wished. Full stop. He has indeed allowed himself to be delayed by pupils who have failed to reach their pick-up point on time, comma, but because of his solicitude the total attendance of pupils from his route has been remarkably high and they do arrive, comma, albeit tardily, comma, in a most cheerful and one thinks therefore receptive state of mind. Full stop. The man has a warmth and interest one would wish to encounter more often in one's staff and I should like to quote [*Fading*] the case of Arthur James Foggon. . . .

Scene: **Inside the bus**   [*Engine idling. Horn sounded: Beep tiddy beeb beeb*]

Girl: Mr Bruin, it's no use waiting. He won't come.

Bruin: Give him time.

Boy: He doesn't come, Mr Bruin, not on Tuesdays.

Girl: Because it's woodwork.

Boy: And he weighs twelve stone.

Girl: And he gave this nail such a belt with the hammer he split the bench in two.

Boy: And the vice went flying through the window of the music room.

Boy and Girl: [*In unison*] And demolished Miss Winkle's piano.

[*We hear a rapid sweep of notes along a piano keyboard, ending in a resonating twang. Many* **Children** *laugh with amusement but also mockingly and with derision*]

Narrator: Poor Fatty Foggon, I think that laugh had mocked him from the day he started school. He lived with his grandparents in a cottage up a muddy lane miles from anywhere so he had no pals from round home and he was no good at lessons or games and even little kids he could have swatted like flies learned to jibe at him before they learned to wipe their snotty noses.

[*Bus horn: Beep tiddy beeb beeb*]

Narrator: His face appeared at his bedroom window, a horrified dumpling, then he swung the curtain back and you could hear the bed springs twang as he leapt under the blankets.

[*Many* **Children**; *a crowing mocking laugh*]

Narrator: But the next Tuesday Fatty Foggon was already in the bus before its first point of call, installed in the seat of honour which everybody wanted beside Mr Bruin.

Girl: How you got there then?

Foggon: He came up for me early. He's going to take me case up.

Scene: **The Headmaster's study**

Bruin: This lad, Headmaster, he's built on the wrong scale for manufacturing tiddling objects like plant-pot stands and book ends.

Headmaster: It's a question of acquiring the facility, Mr Bruin.

Bruin: That's what he has acquired, haven't you, Arthur?

Foggon: What?

Bruin: You've cobbled up a hen cote.

Foggon: With me grandad.

Bruin: And you've erected a fence of railway sleepers.

Foggon: By myself.

Bruin: So if he could be turned to something more on his natural scale.

Headmaster: [*With a laugh*] We've no great pressing need for hen cotes in the school nor fences of railway sleepers. . . .

Bruin: I wasn't suggesting. . . .

Headmaster: Quite so, Bill. Quite so. Could he plane the bottom edge of sticking doors?

Bruin: Could you plane the bottom edge of sticking doors?

Foggon: I could plane the bottom edge of sticking doors.

Headmaster: [*Dictating*] . . . plane the bottom edge of sticking doors. Full stop. The transformation has been remarkable. Full stop. He has become a confident and responsive boy capable of the heavier tasks in joinery and indeed as I look through the window he is at this moment ascending a ladder, comma, hammer in hand, comma, to make good defects in the glass roof of the exterior corridor. Full stop. He has become a most confident and capable craftsman.

[*The crash of a hammer and the shattering of glass*]

Headmaster: Make that, Miss James, *bodes fair* to become a most confident and capable craftsman.

[*The crash of hammer and the shattering of glass*]

Headmaster: [*Shouting above noise*] . . . even if to date his enthusiasm is not quite matched by his skill.

[*The crash of glass*]

Headmaster: Full stop.

Scene: **The bus**

Bruin: Boys and girls, quiet please. If I could just have a word. Now, we have arrived late once or twice of yore.

[*The* Boys, *in high spirits, deny this, shouting, 'No' and 'Never'*]

Bruin: And the Headmaster who is a very reasonable man. . . .

[Boys *repeat their calls of 'No' and 'Never'*]

Bruin: Yes, he is. Has had his bottom kicked by higher authority.

[*The* Boys *laugh*]

Bruin: So we must endeavour to arrive at our ETA of 0850 hours and to make sure we do let's aim for 0845 and everybody be ready starting tomorrow five minutes earlier.

[*The* Boys *groan as the bus moves off*]

Girl: I haven't been late, Mr Bruin.

[*The* Boys *jeer*]

Bruin: You haven't, my dear.

Girl: It's only two people — Charlie Cupboard whose mum wrote up to the Headmaster.

Boy: She didn't.

Girl: Your dad bust the alarm clock and he told my dad he wouldn't buy a new one because it's cheaper to let Mr Bruin hoot.

Boy: You're making it up.

Girl: I'm not. And Fatty Foggon is late because his grandad has a smoke in bed.

Boy: He doesn't, you crow.

Girl: He does, you gobbin. And that day all the smoke was pouring out of the bedroom, well his grandad had gone up in flames and his grandma had beaten him out.

[*The* Boys *laugh and jeer*]

Girl: And another thing, Mr Bruin. You make us late by giving people lifts.

[*The* **Boys** *jeer*]

Bruin: You're quite right, my dear. We must cut that out. Albert, start the cassette.

Cassette: [*Tape gabbles at fast speed and slows to*] . . . pressure 1031 millibars. Our speed is 30 miles an hour . . . [*Tape gabbles fast and slows to*] . . . whose comely daughter, Julie [**Boys** *shout*] is stepping up into the Land-Rover. [**Boys** *whistle*]

[*The tape speeds to a gabble. The bus brakes and stops*]

Bruin: [*Shouts*] Won't it start, Mr Pilchard?

Pilchard: Could you rud be dowd—

Bruin: Certainly, Mr Pilchard.

Girl: Mr Bruin, you said no lifts.

[*The* **Boys** *jeer and one speaks*]

Boy: Shut up, you crow.

Girl: I'm not a crow and he did say no lifts.

Bruin: You're not, my dear, and I did. But this is an exceptional case.

Pilchard: [*Climbing bus steps*] Oh, thak you, Bister Bruid.

[*As the bus moves off* **Bruin** *speaks*]

Bruin: That's a heavy one, Mr Pilchard.

Pilchard: That's be trouble, be double trouble. Be car wote start and be cold wote stop. If you'd just drop be at the road edd.

Bruin: We'll drive you all the way, for what it's worth.

Girl: Mr Bruin, we'll be late.

Bruin: It's only a small detour. We'll make up the time.

Narrator: And we did too. We dropped Mr Pilchard off at the supermarket where he was manager, then out of the little town and back to our route, belting along the straights and sliding round the bends, scattering hens and old ladies and starting stampedes of bullocks in the fields.

[*The bus speeds and rattles along, with rapid gear changes*]

Cassette: [*Played at the fastest speed to remain just intelligible*] Our speed is 70 miles an hour and in a few moments we shall be landing at our destination, the estimable educational establishment of Ernest Epping, Esquire, MA, BSc and bar. We hope you have enjoyed your journey. Please remain in your seats until the engine stops. Thank you.

[*The bus stops with squealing brakes*]

Scene: **The school hall**

Pupils: [*Singing to the piano, with echo*]
'Morning has broken
Like the first morning
Blackbird has spoken
Like the first bird.'

Scene: **The bus**

Narrator: Well, we made it before morning had broken day after day summer and winter, and now Mr Bruin has gone; what's odd when I look back, I never remember a grey ordinary day. I remember days of howling gales and of floods, of still summer mornings when the air shimmered above the radiator and hard evenings in winter when frost sparkled round the street lamps. I remember his laughing red face reflected in his driving mirror and the bus belting along and the children all except this prim girl. . . .

Girl: Mr Bruin, you shouldn't exceed the speed limit because it's against the law.

Narrator: . . . egging him on to a desperate pace to make good the time lost by his ill-considered acts of kindness. We ran Mr Pilchard down to his supermarket whenever he had his double trouble.

Pilchard: Regrettably, Bister Bruid, I ab sibilarly afflicted once bore.

Narrator: We gave the postwoman a lift and the old chap with a leg mounted on an eccentric cam and his uncle and his uncle's pal and his uncle's pal's pig [*Pig grunts*] and the parson and old Mrs Smallwood whose hens we shifted in the boot [*Hens cluck*] and once when her Land-Rover was broken down we even had the personal company of Farmer Snout's comely daughter Julie. [**Boys** *give a deeply appreciative whistle*] Mr Bruin could never bring himself to leave anybody stranded and we had some wild races to make up time.

Boys: [*Shouting*] S-bends, Mr Bruin. Faster.

[*Fast gear change down. Tyres squeal as the bus rattles round bends. The* **Children** *scream with excitement*]

Boys: [*Shouting*] Humped-back bridge, Mr Bruin. Step on it.

[*The* **Children** *scream as the engine roars*]

Boy: Pull the nose up Mr Bruin, and we'll really fly to school.

[*The* **Children** *cheer*]

Scene: **The Education office**

Garbage: Aeronautics are not a part of the syllabus and the drivers of school buses must be instructed to cease, desist and refrain from flying displays. . . .

Narrator: . . . Councillor Garbage told the Education Committee, and continued:

Garbage: Such practices are not conducive to safety.

Scene: **The Headmaster's study**

Headmaster: And they're not, Mr Bruin, they're not. The man's a clown but he has an unassailable point.

Bruin: Yes, Headmaster. Endeavouring to arrive before 'God's recreation'.

Headmaster: But not by throwing all caution to the winds, Mr Bruin. It's a most alarming sight to see pedestrians on all sides leaping for cover as you come rocketing up the street with your tyres smouldering and your windscreen caked with dead flies. See this lady writes:

Woman: It cannot be good for Charlie's head having his thoughts rattled about like this and I am very worried about his future.

Headmaster: What am I to reply, Mr Bruin? I could well say: Have no fears, madam, for Charlie's future. If he continues to travel in Mr Bruin's bus he is unlikely to have one. But is that kind? Is that reassuring to the poor woman?

Bruin: No, Headmaster.

Headmaster: Bill, Councillor Garbage is on our necks, the police have made noises again and the Transport Manager is asking questions — and he's your boss, Bill, not us. He has the final say-so. If you continue to break regulations I shall not be able to defend you.

Bruin: I see that, Ernest.

Headmaster: So no waiting for late pupils, no lifts for unauthorized passengers. Harden your heart, Mr Bruin. Harden your heart.

Narrator: Well, Mr Bruin did to some extent, and its ironical that what led to his downfall was none of the faults the authorities had under scrutiny, though it's true that it all began with giving a lift to Mr Pilchard, but that was strictly only to the road end, not all the way to his supermarket.

Scene: **The bus**

Bruin: Your double trouble again, Mr Pilchard?

Pilchard: Buch worse, Bister Bruid. Trebble trouble. Be car wote start and be cold wote stop and be elephat's handed his cards id.

Bruin: Your elephant?

Girl: A man prances round in an elephant suit and there's a fairy with a wand.

[*The* **Boys** *whistle*]

Pilchard: It's an advertisid probotion.

Bruin: What for?

Pilchard: A rebedy for the cobbod cold.

Bruin: Is it effective?

Pilchard: Bost extrebely so. But these hooligats gave be elephat a goid over and I can't fide another big strog bad.

Boy: You could do it, Mr Bruin.

Pilchard: You're certaidly built for the role, Bister Bruid. If you could see your way to gib be an hour in the biddle of the day. I doe you've been cobbanded to harden your heart but that's only for the jourdeys, isn't it?

Scene: **Outside the supermarket**

Narrator: And so at lunch-time Mr Bruin, affable as ever, appeared outside the supermarket in a plastic elephant suit. Some of us had sneaked out of school to go down. There was a girl who looked frozen stiff dressed as a fairy, and Mr Pilchard read a spiel of which because of his cold only a few words were intelligible.

Pilchard: A sure rebedy for the relief of the cobbod code. The fairy touch with the elephat effect.

Narrator: Very boring; a few gaping women with fags and prams and some old biddies shuffling past without properly stopping to watch. Then suddenly these three yobboes slipped through the crowd and tied Mr Bruin's trunk round a bollard.

[*A crowd of* **Women** *cackle*]

Pilchard: Doe, please boys, dote start on the elephat again.

Narrator: He untethered Mr Bruin's trunk and went back to gabbling through his spiel.

Pilchard: The jumbo size with the elephat effect.

Narrator: And these yobboes slid through again, put Mr Bruin on his back and trussed up his legs with his trunk.

[*The* **Women** *laugh*]

Pilchard: Please lads, please, do dot addoy the elephat.

Narrator: But they had annoyed him and, like many gentle people, Mr Bruin once aroused was very angry indeed. He jerked his trunk free, leapt to his feet and ran amok in the crowd, pummelling people with his paws and cracking them with sideswipes of his plastic trunk. The yobboes ran, but when we went inside to help Mr Bruin out of his elephant suit they nipped in after us, alarming all the shoppers [**Women** *scream*] and in the scuffling Charlie Cupboard had his shirt ripped and two shelves were knocked over, half burying an old lady under an avalanche of falling tins.

[*A clatter of falling tins. The* **Women** *scream*]

Pilchard: Oh, quadruple trouble. Please, boys, please. We're goid to wide up with a stock of dented tids.

Scene: **The town**   [*Various members of the community voice their complaints*]

Woman: Dear Headmaster: Mr Bruin has a lot of influence over the children and he doesn't ought to nurture useless ambitions Charlie now wants nothing but to be an elephant and gives you a mouthful if you say different and the openings are too limited whereas if he kept on more academic lines he could have a shot at all sorts of things and fall back on being a schoolteacher if after all he turns out as thick as his dad now true Mr Bruin has saved us forking out for an alarm clock until you gave him orders otherwise which is quite understood but quite apart from his torn shirt the lady who went down under the peas and peaches was Charlie's grandma's cousin and had brought up a family of twelve all living so I return to my point that being an elephant is a bad example and irresponsible.

Narrator: The word stuck. It stuck fatally.

Man: Irresponsible.

Woman: Most irresponsible.

Man: Utterly irresponsible in every direction. . . .

Narrator: . . . they said at the Parent Teachers' Association, and Councillor Garbage told the Education Committee:

Garbage: It's not one event. He has a persistent record of irresponsibility. We've had complaints from the parents, complaints from the police, complaints from the general public terrorized all along his route and now we have pupils dragged into this ludicrous exhibition. What sort of an example is this to set to schoolchildren? The man is irresponsible and he will have to go.

[**Various voices** *cry, 'Hear, hear'. There is dissent and commotion*]

Scene: **The Headmaster's study**

Bruin: It's no good, Ernest. I will have to go. You'll only jeopardize your own position if you get yourself any further mixed up in this rumpus.

Headmaster: Leave me to look after my position.

Bruin: So long Ernest.

[*Door closes*]

Headmaster: [*Calls*] Mr Bruin. Bill.

Narrator: He caught him at the porch. It was a winter afternoon and Fatty Foggon was fitting a storm guard to the door to cover the gap left by his vigorous planing in the summer.

Headmaster: Bill, I'm most willing to go before them and state a formal case.

Bruin: Bless you, Ernest. But it's time I moved on anyway.

Narrator: Move on? Where to? It was only afterwards we realized how little we knew about him, who he was, where he came from, what he had done before. He took off the cap that was several sizes too small and presented it to the Headmaster.

Bruin: Cheerio, Ernest. Good luck.

Narrator: He passed the empty bus and walked away. The Headmaster turned back into school, saying half to himself and half to Fatty Foggon:

Headmaster: Irresponsible? Is that the kind of man you call irresponsible?

Narrator: And Fatty Foggon, two slow tears on his cheeks, not remotely understanding what the Headmaster was asking, replied:

Foggon: Yes, sir. Yes, sir.

Pupils: [*Sing to piano, with echo*]
'Now the day is over
Night is drawing nigh
Shadows of the evening
Steal across the sky.'

[*The hymn starts under the last part of the speech and emerges into the clear*]

The End

Our Day Out

Willy Russell

Characters

The Teachers:
Mrs Kay (in her early forties)
Susan (early twenties)
Colin (early twenties)
Briggs (early thirties)
Headmaster

The Kids:

Carol (13)	**Andrews** (13)
Reilly (15)	**Ronson** (13)
Digga (15)	**Kevin** (12)
Linda (15)	**Jimmy** (12)
Karen (15)	**Maurice** (12)

Other kids (all around 12 or 13)

Other Adults:

Les, the 'lollipop man'	**John**
The Driver	**Mac**
Mrs Roberts	**Animal Keeper**
Waitress	**Two other Animal Keepers**

First televised on BBC 2, 28 December 1977

Our Day Out

Scene: **In the street**   [*The street is in the inner city of Liverpool. Kids are streaming in one direction. It is approaching 9 a.m. The kids are pushing, shoving, rushing, ambling, leering and jeering. A group of older kids cross the road, ignoring the lollipop man's assistance. He points them out to a passing woman, obviously disgusted.* **Carol** *rushes along the street wearing a school uniform which doubles as a street outfit and her Sunday best. She is eating half a sandwich and clutching a supermarket carrier bag. She arrives at the roadside and, as there isn't a vehicle in sight, goes to cross without bothering to enlist the aid of the lollipop man,* **Les.** *He stops her from stepping off the pavement*]

Les: 'Ey you!

Carol: [*Stopping*] What?

Les: Come here. Come on!

Carol: [*Approaching him*] Agh ey, Les. Come on. I wanna get t' school.

Les: That makes a bloody change.

Carol: We're goin' out. On a trip.

Les: Now listen. Are you listenin'? Y' don't across the road without the assistance of the lollipop man. And that's me!

Carol: There's nott'n comin', though.

Les: Now just you listen; I know it might look as though there's nothin' comin' but how do you know that a truck or car isn't gonna come speedin' out of that side road? Eh?

Carol: [*Looking*] Oh yeh. I never thought of that.

Les: No. I know y' didn't. Y' never do. None of y'. That's why the government hired me to look after y' all.

Carol: Ta Les.

Les: Ey. Where y' goin' today then?

Carol: It's somewhere far away. I forget.

Les: They all goin'?

Carol: Only the kids who go the Progress Class.

Les: What's that?

Carol: What? Y'don't know what the Progress Class is? It's Mrs Kay's class. Y' go down there in the week if y' can't do sums or writing. If y' backward like.

Les: By Christ, I'll bet she's kept busy. They're all bloody backward round here.

Carol: I know. Come on Les. I wanna get there.

[**Les** *looks up and down the road. Not a vehicle in sight*]

Les: Just hold it there.

Carol: There's nott'n comin'.

[**Les** *looks down the road. In the distance a car is just appearing*]

Carol: Oh come on, Les.

[**Les** *holds out his arm to prevent her from crossing. Only when the car is within striking distance does he walk out with his 'Stop' sign. The car pulls to a halt.* **Les** *waves* **Carol** *across*]

Les: [*Quietly to* **Carol** *as she passes*] I got him that time. Arrogant get that one is.

[**Carol** *continues on her way. The driver of the car glares as* **Les** *waves him on*]

Scene: **The school gates**   [*A coach. Various groups of* **Kids** *are scattered near by. One group surrounds a teacher,* **Mrs Kay**, *all of them after her attention. Cries of, 'Miss, miss, miss, me mum said I could go, miss,' and 'Miss, can I come if I haven't got enough money?' and, 'Miss, can I come, miss?'*]

Mrs Kay: All right, all right. Will you just let me have a minute's peace and I'll get you all sorted out. Right. Now those who've got permission to come on the trip but haven't yet paid, I want you to come over here.

[*She moves a short distance away and all the kids follow her.* **Briggs** *surveys this scene*]

Mrs Kay: [*Bright*] Good morning, Mr Briggs.

Briggs: [*Begrudged*] Morning.

[*He turns and enters the school*]

Briggs: [*To a couple of boys*] Come on, move!

Scene: **The Headmaster's office**   [*The* **Headmaster** *is talking to* **Briggs**, *who was the driver of the car*]

Headmaster: Well I'd like you to go with her, John. We can get Frank Collins to take over your examination classes for the

day. I'd just like you to be there and keep an eye on things. I
don't want to be unprofessional and talk about a member of
staff but I get the impression she sees education as one long
game.

Briggs: Well . . . if the antics in her department are anything to
go by. . . ! She always reminds me of a mother hen rather than
a teacher. . . .

Headmaster: Well, anyway, just try and keep things in some
sort of order.

Scene: **The school gates**   [**Mrs Kay** *is talking to two young
teachers,* **Colin** *and* **Susan.** *Around them are excited, lively kids –
not lined up but in random groups*]

Mrs Kay: [*Shouting to a* **Kid**]   Maurice! Come away from that
road will you?

[*The* **Kid** *does so. Two older* **Kids** *come rushing out of school
and up to the* **Teachers**]

Reilly: Miss . . . miss, can we come wit' y'? Can we?

Mrs Kay: Oh, Brian! You know it's a trip for the Progress Class.

Reilly: Agh, ay, miss, we used t' be in the Progress Class though.

Susan: But you're not now, Brian. Now you can read and write
you're back in normal classes.

Mrs Kay: Look Brian. You know I'd take you. But it's not up
to me. Who's your form teacher?

Reilly: Briggsy.

Mrs Kay: Well, you'll have to go and get his permission.

Reilly: [*As he and* **Digga** *rush off*]   You're ace, miss.

Mrs Kay: Brian!

[*He stops*]

Bring a note.

Reilly: [*Worried*] Ah . . . what for, miss?

Mrs Kay: [*Smiling*] Because I wasn't born yesterday, Brian Reilly, and if I don't ask you for a note you'll just hide behind the corner for ten minutes and say he said you could go.

Reilly: [*Knowing she's got him sussed*] As if we'd do a thing like that, miss!

Carol: [*Still tugging*] Where are we goin', miss?

Mrs Kay: Carol . . . Miss Duncan's just told you. Conway. We're going to Conway.

Carol: Miss is that in England, eh?

Colin: It's in Wales, Carol.

Carol: Will we have t' get a boat?

Mrs Kay: Carol . . . we're going on a coach. Look, it's there. You can get on now.

[*She shouts out to the rest of the* **Kids**]

Go on . . . you can all get on now.

[*There is a wild rush of* **Kids** *to the coach doors. The* **Driver** *appears and blocks the way*]

Driver: Right. Just stop there. Don't move.

Kid: Miss said we could get on.

Driver: Oh, did she now?

Kids: Yeh.

Driver: Well, let me tell youse lot something now. Miss isn't the driver of this coach. I am. An' if I say y' don't get on, y' don't get on.

Mrs Kay: Is anything wrong, Driver?

Driver: Are these children in your charge, madam?

Mrs Kay: Yes.

Driver: Well y' haven't checked them, have y'?

Mrs Kay: Checked them? Checked them for what?

Driver: Chocolate an' lemonade! We don't allow it. I've seen it on other coaches madam; fifty-two vomittin' kids . . . it's no joke. No, I'm sorry, we don't allow that.

Mrs Kay: [*To* **Susan**] Here comes Mr Happiness. All right, Driver . . . I'll check for you.

[*To* **Kids**]

. . . Now listen, everyone. If anybody's got any chocolate or lemonade I want you to put your hands up.

[*A sea of dumb faces and unraised hands.* **Mrs Kay** *smiles at the* **Driver**]

There you are, Driver. All right?

Driver: No, it's not all right. Y' can't just take their word for it. They have to be searched. Y' can't just believe kids.

[*Pause.* **Mrs Kay** *stares at him. She could blow up but she doesn't*]

Mrs Kay: Can I have a word with you, Driver, in private?

[*Reluctantly the* **Driver** *gets off the coach and goes across to her. She manouevres it so that he has his back to the coach and the* **Kids**]

What's your name, Driver?

Driver: Me name? I don't usually have to give me name.

Mrs Kay: Oh, come on . . . what's your name?

Driver: Suttcliffe, Ronny Suttcliffe.

Mrs Kay: Well, Ronny, [*Pointing*] take a look up these streets. [*He does and and she motions the other teachers to be getting the* **Kids** *on the coach*] Ronny, would you say they were the sort of streets that housed prosperous parents?

Driver: We usually only do the better schools.

Mrs Kay: All right, you don't like these kids. I can tell that. But do you have to cause them so much pain?

Driver: [*Shocked*] What have I done? I only told 'em to wait. . . .

Mrs Kay: Ronny, the kids with me today don't know what it is to *look* at a bar of chocolate. Lemonade never touches their lips. [*We almost hear the violins*] These are the children, Ronny, who stand outside shop windows in the pouring rain, looking and longing and never getting. Even at Christmas, at Christmas-time when your kids from the better schools are opening presents and singing carols, these kids are left to wander the cold cruel streets.

[*Pause as she sees the effect she is having. The* **Driver** *is grief-stricken*]

Scene: **Inside the coach**   [*The kids are stuffing themselves with sweets and lemonade. The* **Driver** *comes on board and by the time he turns to face the* **Kids** *there is not a bottle of lemonade or chocolate bar in sight. The* **Driver** *puts his hand into his pocket and pulls out a pound note*]

Driver: Here you are, son, [*To* **Kid** *in front seat*] run over to the shops an' get what sweets y' can with that.

[*The* **Kid** *takes the money and gets off the coach.* **Susan,** *the young teacher, leans across to* **Mrs Kay**]

Susan: What did you do?

Mrs Kay: Lied like hell, of course!

[*She gets up and faces the kids*]

Now, will you listen everyone. We'll be setting off for Conway in a couple of minutes.

[*Cheers*]

Now listen! We want everyone to enjoy themselves, so let's have no silly squabbling or doing anything that might be dangerous to yourselves or to others. That's the only rule we have today: think of yourselves, but think of others as well.

[**Reilly** *and* **Digga** *rush into the bus*]

Reilly: Miss, miss, we're comin' wit' y', miss. He said it's all right.

Mrs Kay: Brian, where's the note?

Reilly: He didn't give us one, miss. He's comin' himself. He said to wait.

[**Digga** and **Reilly** *go to the back of the coach.* **Mrs Kay** *looks at* **Colin** *and* **Susan**]

Colin: He's coming to keep an eye on us.

Susan: Make sure we don't enjoy ourselves.

Mrs Kay: Ah well. We'll just have to deal with him the best way we can.

[*She sits down next to* **Carol***. On the back seat of the coach* **Reilly** *and* **Digga** *are facing some small kids*]

Reilly: Right, punks. Move!

Little Kid: Why?

Reilly: Cos we claimed the back seat, that's why.

Little Kid: You're not even in the Progress though.

Digga: We used to be though, so move.

Reilly: Yeh. Respect y' elders!

[*At the front of the coach,* **Briggs** *is climbing aboard. He stands at the front and stares and glares. The* **Kids** *sigh – he is a cloud on the blue horizon*]

Briggs: [*Suddenly barks*] Reilly. Dickson. Sit down!

Reilly: Sir, we was only. . . .

Briggs: [*Staccato*] Sit down, now, come on, move!

[**Reilly** *and* **Digga** *sit on the two small kids who move to make room for them*]

Briggs: Go on, sort yourselves out!

[*He leans across to* **Mrs Kay** *and speaks quietly*]

You've got some real bright sparks here, Mrs Kay. A right bunch.

Mrs Kay: Well, I think we'll be safe now that you've come to look after us.

Briggs: [*Looking at the* **Kids**] There's a few of 'em I could sling off right now.

Mrs Kay: Oh, you are coming with us then?

Briggs: The Boss thought it might be a good idea if you had an extra member of staff.

[*Stands to address the* **Kids**]

Right, listen.

[*Pause*]

We don't want you to think that we don't want you to enjoy yourselves today, because we do! But a lot of you haven't been on a school visit before so you won't know *how* to enjoy yourselves. So I'll tell you. To enjoy a coach trip we sit in our seats. We don't wander up and down the aisle. We talk quietly to our neighbour, not shout at our mates four seats down.

[*Staccato*] Are you listening, girl! We look nicely out of the windows at the scenery. And we don't do anything else.

[*Throughout the speech the* **Kids** *look disappointed*]

Don't worry, I've driven in my car behind school coaches and seen it. A mass of little hands raised in two-fingered gestures to the passing cars. Yes. But we won't do that will we? Will we?

[*Chorus of:* 'No, sir.']

Briggs: No, sir. We won't.

[*The* **Kid** *returning from the shop, armed with sweets, climbs onto the bus*]

Kid: I've got them . . . I've got loads. . . .

Briggs: Where've you been?

Kid: Gettin' sweets, sir.

Briggs: Sweets?

Mrs Kay: [*Reaching for sweets*] Thank you, Maurice.

Briggs: Sweets?

[*The* **Driver** *taps* **Briggs** *on the shoulder*]

Driver: Excuse me, can I have a word with you, please?

Briggs: [*Puzzled*] Yes.

[*The* **Driver** *gets off the coach and* **Briggs** *follows.* **Mrs Kay** *gives the sweets to* **Susan** *who starts to dish them out. We hear a snatch of the* **Driver's** *speech to* **Briggs**]

Driver: The thing is, about these kids, they're like little souls lost an' wanderin' the cruel heartless streets. . . .

[*Inside the coach,* **Colin** *has joined* **Susan** *in giving out the sweets.* **Colin** *is at the back seat*]

Reilly: How y' gettin' on with miss, eh sir?

Digga: We saw y', sir goin' into that pub with her, sir.

[**Susan** *is watching in the background*]

Colin: [*Covering his embarrassment*] Did you?

Reilly: Are you in love with her, sir? Are y'?

Colin: [*Making his escape*] All right . . . you've all got sweets have you?

Reilly: Sir's in love, sir's in love!

[**Reilly** *laughs and jeers as* **Colin** *makes his way down the aisle*]

Susan: Watch it, Brian!

Reilly: [*Feigned innocence*] What?

Susan: You know what.

Reilly: Agh ey, he is in love with y' though, isn't he, miss.

Digga: Miss, I'll bet he wants t' marry y'.

Reilly: You'd be better off with me, miss. I'm better lookin'. An' I'm sexier!

Susan: [*Giving up playing it straight. She goes up to him, leans across and whispers*] Brian . . . little boys shouldn't try to act like men. The day might come when their words are put to the test!

[*She walks away*]

Reilly: [*Jeering*] Any day, miss . . . any day . . . [*Laughs*]

Digga: What did she say? What did she say?

Reilly: Said she fancied me.

[*At the front of the coach,* **Briggs** *and the* **Driver** *are climbing back on board.* **Briggs** *sits opposite* **Mrs Kay**. *He leans across to her*]

Briggs: [*Quietly*] We've got a right head case of a driver.

[*The engine roars into life. The* **Kids** *cheer.* **Briggs** *turns round with a warning look as the coach pulls away from the school. Thousands of little fingers raise in a V-sign out of the windows*]

Scene: **Leaving the city**   [*As the coach goes along the city streets the* **Kids** *are talking and laughing and pointing. On the back seat,* **Reilly** *secretly takes out a packet of Number Six cigarettes. The* **Little Kid** *sees them*]

Digga: Reilly, light up.

Reilly: Where's Briggsy?

Digga: He's at the front, I'll keep dixie. Come on, we're all right, light up.

Little Kid: Agh 'ey. You've got ciggies. I'm gonna tell miss.

Reilly: Shut up you an' open that friggin' window.

Little Kid: No . . . I'm gonna tell miss.

Digga: Go'n tell her. She won't do nott'n anyway.

Kid: I'll tell sir.

Reilly: You do an' I'll gob y'.

Digga: Come on . . . open that window, you.

Kid: Why?

Reilly: Why d' y' think? So we get a bit of fresh air.

Kid: Well there's no fresh air round here. You just wanna smoke. An' smokin' stunts y' growth.

Reilly: I'll stunt your friggin' growth if y' don't get it open.

[**Andrews** *gets up and reaches for the window*]

Andrews: I'll open it for y' Reilly.

[**Reilly** *ducks behind the seat and lights up*]

Andrews: Gis a ciggy.

Reilly: Get y' own ciggies.

Andrews: Ah go on. I opened the window for y'.

Digga: Y' can buy one off us.

Andrews: I can't. I haven't got any money.

Reilly: Course y've got money.

Andrews: Me ma wouldn't give me any. She didn't have any.

Digga: Go 'way . . . your ma's loaded.

Andrews: No she's not.

Reilly: Well she should be . . . all the fellers she picks up on Parly.

Andrews: Go on . . . gis a ciggy.

Digga: She's always with the blacks off the boats, your ma. And they're loaded, them blacks are.

Reilly: An you must have money cos they pay a fortune for a bit of White.

Andrews: Well *I've* got no money . . . honest.

Digga: Well, y've got no ciggies either.

Andrews: I'll give y' half me sarnies for one ciggie.

Reilly: What's on 'em?

Andrews: Jam.

Reilly: I hate jam.

[*They have become lax about keeping an eye out and do not notice* **Briggs** *getting up from his seat and approaching the back of the coach.* **Digga** *suddenly looks up and sees him*]

Digga: Briggs!

[**Reilly** *passes the cigarette to* **Andrews**]

Reilly: Here!

Andrews: Ta.

[**Andrews** *takes it and, making sure that his head is out of sight, he takes a huge drag. When he looks up,* **Briggs** *is peering down at him*]

Briggs: Put it out!

Andrews: Sir, sir, I wasn't. . . .

Briggs: Put it out. Now get to the front of the coach.

Andrews: Sir, I was just. . . .

Briggs: I said get to the front!

[**Andrews** *sighs, gets up and goes to the front of the coach.* **Briggs** *sits in* **Andrew's** *seat*]

Briggs: Was it your ciggie, Reilly?

Reilly: Sir, I swear on me mother.

Digga: Don't believe him, sir. How can he swear on his mother. She's been dead for ten years.

Briggs: All right, all right. We don't want any argument. There'll be no more smoking if I stay up here, will there?

[**Carol,** *who is sitting next to* **Mrs Kay,** *is staring out of the window*]

Carol: Isn't it horrible, eh, miss.

Mrs Kay: Mm?

Carol: Y' know . . . all the thingy like. The dirt an' that.
[*Pause*] I like them nice places.

Mrs Kay: Which places?

Carol: Y' know them places on the telly. Where they have gardens an' trees outside an' that.

Andrews: Sir, sir, I can't.

Briggs: Thirteen and you can't stop smoking!

Andrews: No, sir.

Briggs: [*Sighing, shaking his head*] Well you'd better not let me catch you again.

Andrews: No, sir, I won't.

[*Pause as they each go into their respective thoughts.* **Briggs** *turns and looks at* **Mrs Kay**. *She looks at him and smiles warmly. He tries to respond but doesn't quite make it.* **Colin** *walks along the aisle generally checking that everything is all right. As he gets near* **Linda**'s *seat her friend,* **Karen**, *taps her and points him out.* **Linda** *immediately turns round and smiles at* **Colin**. *It's obvious that she fancies him*]

Linda: Sir, y' comin' to sit by me are y'?

Karen: [*On the seat behind* **Linda**] Don't sit by her, sir . . . come an' sit by me.

Colin: I've got a seat at the front, thanks.

Linda: 'Ey, sir.

Colin: What, Linda?

Linda: Come here, I wanna tell y' somethin'.

Colin: Well, go on.

Linda: Ah ey sir, I don't want everyone to hear. Come on, just sit down here while I tell y'.

Karen: Go on, sir . . . she won't harm y'.

Linda: Come on, sir.

[*Reluctantly* **Colin** *sits by her.* **Karen**'s *head is poking through the space between the seats and both girls laugh*]

Colin: What is it?

[*They laugh*]

You're not goin' to tell me a joke, are you?

[*The girls laugh even more*]

Well, I'll have to go.

[**Linda** *quickly links her arm through his and holds him there*]

Linda: No, sir . . . listen. Listen, she said, I wouldn't tell y' . . . but I will. [*Pause*] Sir, I think you're lovely.

Colin: [*Quickly getting up. Embarrassed*] Linda!

[*He walks away from the girls to the back of the coach*]

Linda: I told him. I said I would. Ooh . . . he's ace isn't he?

Karen: You've got no chance. He's goin' with miss.

Linda: I know. [*Pause*] He might chuck her though an' start goin' with me. He might marry me.

Karen: [*Shrieking*] Ooer! Don't be stupid, you. You won't get a husband like sir. You'll end up marryin' someone like your old feller.

Linda: You're just jealous you, girl.

Karen: Aaght.

[**Colin** *talks to the lads on the back seat.* **Reilly** *hides a cigarette in his cupped hand*]

Colin: All right lads . . . it shouldn't be too long before we're getting into Wales.

Little Kid: That's in the country, Wales, isn't it, sir?

Colin: A lot of it is countryside, yes.

Reilly: Lots of woods, eh sir?

Colin: Woods and mountains, lakes . . .

Reilly: You gonna take miss into the woods, are y', sir?

Colin: [*Pause*] Now just watch it, Brian, all right?

Reilly: Sir, I just meant was y' gonna show her the trees an' the plants. . . .

Colin: I know quite well what you meant.

[*Turns to go*]

And if I was you I'd put that fag out before you burn your hand. If Mr Briggs sees that you'll be spending the rest of the day alongside him. Now come on, put it out.

[**Reilly** *takes a last mammoth drag and then stubs out the cigarette.* **Colin** *walks back along the aisle*]

Reilly: [*Shouting after him*] I'll show her the woods for y', sir.

[**Colin** *pretends not to hear.* **Reilly** *leans across to the* **Little Kid** *in the seat in front and knocks him*]

Reilly: Give us a sweet you, greedy guts.

Kid: I've only got a few left.

Digga: You've got loads.

Kid: I haven't.

Reilly: Let's have a look then.

[*The* **Kid** *falls for it and shows him the bag.* **Reilly** *snatches it*]
Ta!

Scene: **In the country** [*The coach is on a country road.* **Mrs Kay** *is talking to the* **Driver**]

Mrs Kay: Ronny, I was just wondering, is there somewhere round here we could stop and let the kids stretch their legs a bit?

Driver: Well I'll tell y' what, Mrs Kay, there's a few cafés a bit
further on. D' y' want me to pull into one of them?

Mrs Kay: Smashing.

Scene: **A roadside café**   [*Outside the café there are signs saying: 'Open' and 'Coaches Welcome'. Inside the café, a* **Waitress** *is
working on the tables. There is also a woman,* **Mrs Roberts,** *working behind the counter*]

Waitress: [*Looking up and seeing coach in distance*] Better be
getting some cups ready, Mrs Roberts. There's a coach comin'.

Mrs Roberts: [*Moving over to window*] Where is it?

Waitress: Probably pensioners so early in the season.

Mrs Roberts: [*Worried*] No. I don't . . . I don't think so.

[*She moves behind the counter and produces a pair of binoculars*]

Let me see.

[*She lifts the binoculars and looks at the coach. She can see
the kids and the destination indicator which reads: 'Liverpool
to Conway'. She lowers the binoculars and frowns a worried
frown*]

Right! Come on, action!

Scene: **Inside the coach**   [**Mr Briggs** *is addressing the* **Kids**]

Briggs: Now the folk who run these places provide a good and
valuable service to travellers like us . . . so remember what I've
said.

Scene: **Back at the café**   [*The café is alive with activity: the shutters are coming down, the 'Coaches Welcome' sign is replaced by 'Absolutely no Coaches' and the 'Open' sign by one saying 'Closed'. The doors are locked and bolted;* **Mrs Roberts** *and the* **Waitress** *lean against the door*]

Scene: **In the coach**   [*The coach has pulled up. The* **Driver** *and* **Mrs Kay** *are looking at the café*]

Mrs Kay: Perhaps it's because it's so early in the season. Maybe if they knew there was the chance of some business they'd open for us. I'll go and give them a knock.

Scene: **In the café**   [*Inside, the two women are silent, terrified. They hear footsteps coming up the drive. The door is knocked upon.* **Mrs Kay** *is on the other side of the door watched by the* **Kids** *from the coach windows. She knocks again*]

Mrs Roberts: [*From within*] We are closed!
Mrs Kay: You couldn't possibly. . . .
Mrs Roberts: [*Firm*] We are closed.

  [**Mrs Kay** *moves away. As the two women hear the receding footsteps, they sigh*]
Mrs Roberts: I only ever did it once, take a Liverpool coach load. I tell you not one word of a lie Miss Powell, they'd rob your eyes if you wasn't lookin'.

  [*The coach pulls away. The* **Kids** *give V-signs to the café and cross their legs to stop themselves from wetting*]

Scene: **A café and shop**   [*On the window a sign reads: 'Under New Management'. Inside, two men,* **John** *and* **Mac**, *are behind the counter generally preparing their place for the season*]

John: Look, how many times, listen, it's only the start of the season innit? Eh? Course it is. We can't make a bloody fortune before the season's begun, can we?

Mac: See, it's no that what's worryin' me. What I think, see, is we bought the wrong place. If you was askin' me, I'd say the coaches'll stop at the first café they come to. An' that's up the road.

John: Some of them will, yeh. But there'll be enough for us as well. Give it a month, that's all; y' won't be able t' see this road for coaches. Thousands of schoolkids with money t' burn. We'll clean up, mate.

[*They hear the sound of brakes and of tyres pulling up.* **John** *looks out of the window*]

Now what did I say, eh?

Mac: [*Looking out of window. Brightening*] Look at that. Christ, there's hundreds of them.

John: Right. Let's go. Come on.

[*Moves to the counter and points out the items quickly*]

John: Jelly Babies: fifteen p. a quarter.

Mac: I thought they was only twelve.

John: Ice creams nine p.

Mac: They was only seven p. yesterday.

John: Listen, mate, can I help inflation?

Mac: [*Getting the picture*] Oh right. I get the picture.

John: Passin' trade mate. Always soak the passin' trade. Y' never see them again so it don't matter. Bubble Gum two p. — no, make that three. Ice lollies ten p. Come on . . . get those doors open. We'll milk this little lot.

Scene: **In the car park**   [*The* **Kids** *are tumbling off the coach.* **Mrs Kay** *takes out a flask and sits on a bench in the café garden.* **Briggs** *is frantic*]

Briggs: Stop! Slater, walk . . . walk! You, boy . . . come here. Now stop. All of you . . . stop!

Mrs Kay: [*Pouring out coffee*] Mr Briggs, they'll. . . .

Briggs: [*To a boy,* **Ronson**, *who is rushing for the door of the shop*] Ronson! Come here!

[**Ronson** *stops and walks back to* **Briggs**, *shrugging*]

Mrs Kay: Mr Briggs . . . as long as they don't go near the road I don't think there's any. . . .

Briggs: All right, Mrs Kay.

[**Ronson** *stands in front of him*]

Now just where do you think you are?

[**Ronson** *is puzzled*]

Well?

[**Ronson** *looks round for help in answering. There is none*]

Ronson: [*Sincerely*] Sir, Wales?

Scene: **Inside the shop**   [*The counter cannot be seen for pushing, impatient* **Kids**. *The two men are working frantically as orders are fired at them from all quarters. As the orders are shouted, the*

Kids are robbing stuff left, right and centre — it's the usual trick but the two men are falling for it — the **Kids** *point to jars high up, as the men turn their backs, so racks of chocolate bars disappear into eager pockets*]

Scene: **Outside the shop**

Briggs: And don't let me catch you at it again. Now go on. Walk.

[*He watches as* **Ronson** *walks into the shop. Satisfied, he turns to* **Mrs Kay**]

Now, Mrs Kay, what was it you wanted?

Mrs Kay: Well, I just thought you might like to have a sit down away from them for a few minutes.

Briggs: To be quite honest, Mrs Kay. I think we should all be inside, looking after them. Do you think it was wise just letting them all pour in there at once?

Mrs Kay: Ooh ... leave them. They've been cooped up for over an hour. They'll want to stretch their legs and let off a bit of steam.

Briggs: I don't mind them stretching their legs. It's not the children I'm concerned about.

Mrs Kay: Well, just who are you concerned about?

Briggs: There's not only our school to think about, you know. There's others who come after us and they're dependent upon the goodwill of the people who run these places.

Mrs Kay: [*Pouring out another cup of coffee*] Considering the profit they make out of the kids I don't think they've got much to complain about.

Briggs: [*Taking cup*] Thanks. [*Pause*] You know, I'll have to

say this to you, Mrs Kay, there are times when I really think
you're on their side.

[*Pause*]

Mrs Kay: And I'll have to say this to you, Mr Briggs, I didn't
ask you to come on this trip.

Briggs: No, but the Headmaster did.

Scene: **Outside the coach**   [*The last few stragglers climb on
board*]

Mrs Kay: [*To the* **Kids**] Are you the last? Anyone left in the
toilet?

Susan: [*As she finishes counting heads*] That's the lot. We've
got them all.

Mrs Kay: All right Ron.

Driver: Right love. [*Starts engine*]

Scene: **In the shop**   [*The* **Kids** *have gone and the shelves are
almost bare. The two men sit back, exhausted but satisfied*]

Mac: If I hadn't seen it with m' own eyes.

John: I told y'.

Mac: We'll have to re-order.

John: An' that's just one coachload.

Mac: We must've took a bloody fortune.

John: There was sixty quid's worth of stock on those shelves
an' most of it's gone.

Mac: Come . . . let's count up.

[*He gets up, goes to the till and opens it. It contains a lot of change but hardly any notes. He is puzzled*]

Was you lookin' after the notes?

John: Which notes? I thought you was takin' care of them.

Mac: Well, we must of taken a load of notes.

[*He looks at the bare shelves*]

Scene: **Inside the coach**   [*The* **Kids** *are weighed down with sweets*]

Scene: **The shop**

Mac: The thievin' little bastards!

[*He rushes for the door.* **John** *follows. As he flings back the door he sees the coach just pulling away down the road. They run after the disappearing coach. The back window is a mass of two-fingered gestures. The two men are finally left standing in the road*]

Scene: **In the coach**   [**Mrs Kay** *leaves her seat and goes over to* **Susan**'s *seat.* **Susan** *is playing 'I Spy' with a couple of girls who are sitting with her*]

[**Briggs** *moves across to talk to* **Colin.** *He is conspiratorial*]

Briggs: You know what her problem is, don't you?

Colin: [*Trying to keep out of it. Looking out of window*] Mm?

Briggs: Well, she thinks I can't see through all this woolly-headed liberalism, you know what I mean? I mean, all right, she has her methods, I have mine but I can't see why she has to set herself up as the great champion of the non-academics. Can you? It might look like love and kindness but if you ask me I don't think it does the kids a scrap of good.

Colin: Erm. . . .

Briggs: I mean, I think you have to risk being disliked if you're going to do any good for these type of kids. They've got enough freedom at home, haven't they, with their two quid pocket money and television till all hours, haven't they? [*Pause*] I don't know what you think but I think her philosophy is totally confused. What do you think?

[**Briggs** *waits for an answer*]

Colin: Actually, I don't think it's got anything to do with a philosophy.

Briggs: What? You mean you haven't noticed all this, sort of, anti-establishment, let the kids roam wild, don't check them attitude?

Colin: Of course I've noticed it. But she's like that all the time. This trip isn't organized according to any startling theory.

Briggs: Well what is the method she works to then? I mean, you tell me, you know her better than I do.

Colin: The only principle behind today is that the kids should have a good day out.

Briggs: Well that's all I'm saying, but if they're going to have a good and stimulating day then it's got to be planned and executed better than this.

[*While* **Briggs** *is talking,* **Mrs Kay** *has moved to have a word with the* **Driver**. *Suddenly the coach swings into a driveway.* **Briggs** *is startled and puzzled*]

What's this . . . where are we. . . .

Mrs Kay: It's all right, Mr Briggs ... I've checked it with the Driver. I thought it would be a good idea if we called into the zoo for an hour. We've got plenty of time.

Briggs: But I thought this trip was organized so that the kids could see Conway Castle.

Mrs Kay: We'll be going to the castle after. [*To the* **Kids**] Now listen, everybody. As a sort of extra bonus, we've decided to call in here and let you have an hour at the zoo.

[*Cheers*]

Briggs: Look, we can't. . . .

Mrs Kay: Now the rest of the staff and myself will be around if you want to know anything about the animals — mind you, there's not much point in asking me, because I don't know one monkey from the next.

Reilly: [*Shouting from back*] Apart from Andrews, miss, he's a gorilla.

[**Andrews** *gives him a V-sign*]

Mrs Kay: And yourself, Brian, the Oorang Utang.

[*The* **Kids** *laugh.* **Reilly** *waves his fist*]

Digga: Don't worry, miss, he's a big baboon.

Mrs Kay: Now let's not have any silly name-calling.

Briggs: [*Whispering in* **Mrs Kay's** *ear*] Mrs Kay. . . .

Mrs Kay: [*Ignoring him*] Now as I was saying, I don't know a great deal about the animals but we're very lucky to have Mr Briggs with us because he's something of an expert in natural history. So, if any of you want to know more about the animals you see, Mr Briggs will tell you all about them. Come on, leave your things on the coach.

Kid: Agh, great.

[*The* **Kids** *begin to get up*]

Scene: **The zoo**   [*The* **Kids** *wander around in groups – pulling faces at the animals, pointing and running, girls walking arm in arm. They point and shriek with horrified delight at the sexual organs of monkeys.* **Mr Briggs** *is with a group of* **Kids** *looking at a large bear in a pit*]

Briggs: . . . and so you can see with those claws it could give you a very nasty mark.

Andrews: An' could it kill y', sir?

Briggs: Well, why do you think it's kept in a pit?

Ronson: I think that's cruel. Don't you?

Briggs: No. Not if it's treated well. And don't forget it was born in captivity so it won't know any other sort of life.

Ronson: I'll bet it does, sir.

Girl 1:   How do you know? Sir's just told y' hasn't he? If it was born in a cage an' it's lived all its life in a pit, well, it won't know nothin' else so it won't want nothin' else, will it?

Ronson: Well, why does it kill people then?

Andrews: What's that got to do with it?

Ronson: It kills them cos they're cruel to it. They keep it in a pit so when it gets out it's bound to be mad an' wanna kill people. Don't you see?

Andrews: Sir, he's thick. Tell him to shurrup, sir.

Ronson: I'm not thick. If it lived there all its life it must know, mustn't it, sir?

Briggs: Know what?

Andrews: Sir, he's nuts.

Ronson: It must know about other ways of living, sir. Y' know, free, like the way people have stopped it livin'. It only kills people cos it's trapped an' people are always stood lookin' at it. If it was free it wouldn't bother people at all.

Briggs: Well, I wouldn't be so sure about that, Ronson.

Andrews: Sir's right. Bears kill y' cos it's in them t' kill y'.

Girl 2:   Agh come on, sir . . . let's go to the Children's Zoo.

Andrews: Let's go to the big ones.

Briggs: It's all right . . . we'll get round them all eventually.

Girl 1:   Sir, we goin' the Children's Zoo then.

Briggs: If you want to.

Girl 1:   Come on.

[**Briggs** *starts to walk away. The two girls link his arms, one on either side. He stops*]

Briggs: Oh! [*Taking their arms away*] Walk properly.

Girl 2:   Agh ey, sir, the other teachers let y' link them.

[**Mrs Kay** *is with another group. She sees* **Briggs**]

Mrs Kay: Oh hello. How are you getting on? They plying you with questions?

Briggs: Yes, they've been very good.

Mrs Kay: I'm just going for a cup of coffee. Do you want to join me?

Briggs: Well I was just on my way to the Children's Zoo with these.

Andrews: It's all right, sir. We'll go on our own.

Mrs Kay: Oh come on. They'll be all right.

Briggs: Well, I don't know if these people can be trusted on their own, Mrs Kay.

Mrs Kay: It's all right, Susan and Colin are walking round and the place is walled in. They'll be all right.

Andrews: Go on, sir. You go an' get a cuppa. Y' can trust us.

Briggs: Ah! Can I though? If I go off for a cup of coffee with Mrs Kay can you people be trusted to act responsibly?

[*Chorus of 'Yes, sir'*]

Briggs: All right Mrs Kay. We'll trust them to act responsibly.

Mrs Kay: Come on.

[*They walk off to the zoo café*]

Scene: **The bird house** [*Two boys are slowly repeating, 'Everton, Everton' to two blue and yellow macaws*]

Boy: Go on, just tweek it out, you dislocated sparrow . . . speak!

Scene: **The children's zoo** [*The Kids watch a collection of small animals – rabbits, gerbils, guinea pigs, bantam hens – all contained in an open pit.* **Ronson** *looks fondly at a rabbit*]

Ronson: They're great, aren't they?

Carol: They're lovely.

Ronson: [*Bending over and stroking a rabbit*] Come on . . . come on. . . .

Carol: Ey' you. Y' not supposed t' touch them.

[**Ronson** *answers by picking up the rabbit and gently stroking it.* **Carol** *reaches over to join him stroking the rabbit but he pulls it close to him protectively*]

Carol:　Well. I'll get one of me own.

[*She bends down and picks up a guinea pig which she strokes affectionately*]

These are better anyway!

Scene:　**The zoo café**　[**Mr Briggs** *and* **Mrs Kay** *are waiting for coffee at the service rail*]

Briggs:　How many sugars, Mrs Kay?

Mrs Kay:　Call me Helen. I hate being called Mrs Kay all the time. Makes me feel old. I tried to get the kids to call me Helen once. I had the class full of chanting it. Two minutes later they were calling me Mrs Kay again. No, no sugar, thank you.

Scene:　**The children's zoo**　[*More* **Kids** *have followed* **Ronson's** *example. Quite a few of them are now clutching furry friends*]

Carol:　I'm gonna call mine Freddy. Hiya, Freddy. Hello, Freddy. Freddy.

Scene:　**The zoo café**　[**Mrs Kay** *and* **Briggs** *are sitting at a table; she lights a cigarette*]

Briggs:　They're really interested, you know, really interested in the animals.

Mrs Kay:　I thought they'd enjoy it here.

Briggs: Perhaps when we're back in school we could arrange something; maybe I could come along and give them a small talk with some slides that I've got.

Mrs Kay: [*Enthusiastic*] Oh, would you?

Briggs: You should have asked me to do something a long time ago.

Mrs Kay: Well, don't forget you've never offered before.

Briggs: To tell you the truth I didn't think the kids who came to you would be too interested in animals.

Scene: **The children's zoo**   [*The animal pit is empty. The children have gone*]

Scene: **The coach**   [**Briggs** *and* **Mrs Kay** *approach*]

Briggs: Don't worry, we'll get that arranged as soon as we get back to school.

[**Susan** *and* **Colin** *stand by the coach with the* **Driver**]

Colin: [*To* **Driver**] You should have come round with us, it's a grand zoo.

Driver: A couple of hours kip — seen it all before.

Colin: You'd have had a good time.

Mrs Kay: All on board?

Susan: Yes. We wandered back and most of them were already here.

Mrs Kay: Oh! That makes a change.

Briggs: All checked and present. Right. Off we go.

[*The* **Driver** *and the teachers climb on board. In the distance* *the* **Animal Keeper**, *polo-necked and wellied, runs towards the coach. Inside the coach the* **Kids** *sit like angels. The coach pulls away but the* **Animal Keeper** *waves it down. It stops. The* **Keeper** *strides on board*]

Mrs Kay: Have we forgotten something?

Keeper: Are you supposed to be in charge of this lot?

Mrs Kay: Why? What's that matter?

Keeper: Children. They're not bloody children. They're animals. That's not a zoo out there. This is the bloody zoo, in here!

Briggs: Would you mind controlling your language and telling me what's going on.

Keeper: [*Ignoring him and pushing past him to the* **Kids**] Right. Come on. Where are they?

[*The* **Kids** *look back innocently*]

Call yourselves teachers. You can't even control them.

Briggs: Now look. This has just gone far enough. Would you tell me exactly what you want please?

[*A clucking hen is heard. The* **Keeper** *turns and looks. A* **Kid** *is fidgeting with his coat. The* **Keeper** *strides up to him and pulls back his coat, revealing a bantam hen. Two more* **Keepers** *come on board. The first* **Keeper** *grabs the hen and addresses the* **Kids**]

Keeper: Right! And now I want the rest!

[*There is a moment's hesitation before the flood-gates are opened. Animals appear from every conceivable hiding place. The coach becomes a menagerie.* **Mrs Kay** *raises her eyebrows to heaven. The* **Keepers** *collect the animals.* **Briggs** *stares icily*]

Scene: **The coach, moments later**   [**Briggs** *is outside talking* *to the* **Keepers**, *who have collected all the animals in small cages. They walk away and* **Briggs** *climbs onto the coach. His face is like thunder. The* **Kids** *try to look anywhere but at him — trying to avoid the unavoidable.* **Briggs** *pauses for a long, staring, angry and contemptuous moment*]

Briggs: I trusted you lot. [*Pause*] I trusted you. And this, is the way you repay me. [*Pause*] I trusted all of you, but it's obvious that trust is something you know nothing about.

Ronson: Sir, we only borrowed them.

Briggs: [*Shouting*] Shut up, lad! [*Pause*] Is it any wonder that people won't do anything for you? The minute we start to treat you as real people, what happens? That man was right, you act like animals, animals! [*Pause*] Well I've learned a lesson today. Oh, yes, I have. I've learned that trust is something you people don't understand. Now, I'm warning you, all of you, don't expect any more trust from me!

[*The* **Kids** *are resigned. They have heard it all before.* **Briggs** *turns to* **Mrs Kay**]

Mrs Kay. When we get to the castle we'll split up into four groups. Each member of staff will be responsible for one group.

[**Mrs Kay** *looks at him*]

Scene: **Conway Castle** [**Briggs**, *with a group of ordered children standing behind him, points to a spot high up on the castle. The* **Kids** *all look up, bored*]

Briggs: Now you see these larger square holes, just below the battlements there — well, they were used for ... long planks of wood which supported a sort of platform, and that's where the archers used to stand and fire down on the attackers of the castle. Now what's interesting is, if you look at the side of that tower it's not quite perpendicular. What's perpendicular mean?

Milton: Sir, sir.

Briggs: All right, Milton.

Milton: Straight up, sir. [*Sniggers from the other boys*]

[*In another part of the castle,* **Kids** *are rushing about playing medieval cowboys and Indians.* **Mrs Kay** *sits on a bench overlooking the estuary.* **Carol** *and* **Andrews** *are with her. In a secluded passage of the castle,* **Reilly** *and* **Digga** *are smoking; they are concealed in an alcove.* **Colin's** *voice can be heard. He approaches,* **Karen** *and* **Linda** *follow close behind him*]

Colin: So, although these walls are nearly fifteen feet thick in places, you still have the wind blasting in through the arrow slits and with no proper heat, you can imagine just how cold it must have been.

Linda: Sir, I wonder what they did to keep warm in the olden days?

Colin: [*Stopping and turning*] Well, obviously they. . . . Where's everybody else gone? Where are the others?

Karen: Sir, they kept dropping out as you were talkin'.

Colin: Oh God.

Linda: It's all right, sir. Y' can keep showin' us round. We're dead interested.

Colin: [*Sighing*] All right Linda . . . what was I saying?

Linda: Sir, y' was tellin' us how they kept warm in the olden days.

Colin: [*Continuing down the passage*] They wore much thicker clothing . . . All right, Linda?

Linda: Sir, it's dead spooky. It's haunted isn't it?

Colin: Don't be silly.

Linda: Sir, I'm frightened [*Linking his arm for protection*]

Colin: Now, don't do that, Linda!

Linda: [*Holding on*] But I'm frightened, sir.

Karen: [*Grabbing his other arm*] Sir, so am I.

Colin: [*Firmly, freeing himself*] Now, girls, stop being silly. Stop it. There's nothing to be frightened of! Now, come on.

[*He leads them along the passage. As they pass the alcove where* **Reilly** *and* **Digga** *are concealed,* **Reilly** *leans out and just gently touches* **Linda's** *shoulder. She screams and flings herself at* **Colin**, **Karen** *reacts and does the same. Even* **Colin** *is slightly startled*]

Linda: Sir, it touched me.

Colin: What did?

Linda: Oh, it did.

[**Colin** *looks worried. They hear laughter. Just at the point when the three of them are about to run,* **Reilly** *and* **Digga** *fall laughing out of the alcove. In the distance* **Briggs** *shouts, 'Reilly!'* **Reilly** *and* **Digga** *hear him and leg away past* **Colin** *and the terrified girls. Outside,* **Mrs Kay**, **Carol** *and* **Andrews** *still sit looking out over the estuary*]

Mrs Kay: Why don't you go and have a look around the castle grounds. You haven't seen it yet.

Carol: Miss, I don't like it. It's horrible. I just like sittin' here with you, lookin' at the lake.

Mrs Kay: That's not a lake, love. It's the sea.

Carol: That's what I meant, miss.

Andrews: Miss, wouldn't it be great if we had something like this round ours. Then the kids wouldn't get into trouble if they had somewhere like this to play, would they?

Carol: Miss. Couldn't have nothin' like this round our way could they?

Mrs Kay: Why not?

Carol: Cos we'd only wreck it, wouldn't we?

Andrews: No, we wouldn't.

Carol: We would, y' know. That's why we never have nothin' nice round our way − cos we'd just smash it up. The Corpy knows that so why should they waste their money, eh? They'd give us things if we looked after them, but we don't look after them, do we?

Andrews: Miss, miss, y' know what I think about it, eh, miss.

Mrs Kay: Go on, John. What do you think?

Andrews: Miss, if all this belonged to us, miss, and it was ours, not the Corpy's but, ours, well, we wouldn't let no one wreck it would we? We'd defend it.

[**Briggs** *approaches, obviously angry*]

Briggs: You two . . . off! Go on. Move.

Carol: Sir, where?

Briggs: Anywhere, girl. Just move. I want to speak to Mrs Kay. Well, come on then.

[*The two kids,* **Carol** *and* **Andrews***, wander off.* **Briggs** *waits until they are out of hearing range*]

Mrs Kay: I was talking to those children.

Briggs: Yes, and I'm talking to you, Mrs Kay. It's got to stop, this has.

Mrs Kay: What has?

Briggs: What has? Can't y' see what's goin' on? It's a shambles, the whole ill-organised affair. Look at what they did at the zoo. Just look at them here.

[*All around the castle they can see, from where they sit,* **Kids** *running, pulling, laughing and shouting*]

They're just left to race and chase and play havoc. God knows what the castle authorities must think. Look, when you bring children like ours into this sort of environment you can't afford to just let them go free. They're just like town dogs let off the lead in the country. My God, for some of them it's the first time they've been further than Birkenhead.

Mrs Kay: [*Quietly*] I know. And I was just thinking; it's a shame really, isn't it, eh? You know, we bring them to a crumbling pile of bricks and mortar and they think they're in the fields of heaven.

[*Pause. He glares at her*]

Briggs: [*Accusing*] You *are* on their side aren't you?

Mrs Kay: [*Looking at him*] Absolutely, Mr Briggs. Absolutely!

Briggs: Look! All I want to know from you is what you're going to do about this chaos.

Mrs Kay: Well, I'd suggest that if you want the chaos to stop, then you should stop seeing it as chaos. All right, the Head-master asked you to come along — but can't you relax? There's no point in pretending that a day out to Wales is going to fur-nish them with the education they should have had long ago. It's too late for them. Most of them were rejects on the day they were born, Mr Briggs. We're not going to solve anything today. Can't we just try and give them a good day out? At least we could try and do that.

Briggs: [*The castle looming behind him*] Well, that's a fine attitude isn't it? That's a fine attitude for a member of the teaching profession to have.

Mrs Kay: [*Beginning to lose her temper ever so slightly*] Well, what's your alternative? Eh? Do you really think there's any point pretending? Even if you cared do you think you could educate these kids, my remedial kids? Because you're a fool if you do. You won't educate them because nobody wants them educating. . . .

Briggs: Listen Mrs Kay. . . .

Mrs Kay: No! You listen, Mr Briggs. . . . If these kids, and all the others like them, had real learning the factories of England would empty overnight. And don't you try and tell me that there's kids who, given the choice, would still empty bins and stand on production lines, but don't give me that because that's the biggest myth of all. Give them education – choice – and they'd want what we've got, what the best-off have got. And that's why you won't educate them, Mr Briggs. You're in a job that's designed to fail, because no matter what the rest of us want, the factories of England must have their fodder.

Briggs: And I suppose that's the sort of stuff you've been pumping into their minds, is it?

Mrs Kay: [*Laughing*] And you really think they'd understand?

Briggs: Listen, I'm not going to spend any more time arguing with you. You may have organized this visit, but I'm the one who's been sent by the Headmaster to supervise. Now, either you take control of the children in your charge or I'll be forced to abandon this visit and order everyone home.

[*Pause. She looks at him*]

Mrs Kay: Well . . . that's your decision. But I'm not going to let you prevent the kids from having some fun. If you want to abandon this visit then you'd better start walking because we're not going home. We're going to the beach.

Briggs: The beach!!

Mrs Kay: We can't come all the way to the seaside and not go down to the beach!

[*She turns and walks away*]

Scene: **The beach** [**Briggs** *sits on a rock apart from the main group.* **Mrs Kay** *is paddling, dress held above her knees looking old-fashioned, with a group of kids. Girls are screaming in delight and boys are laughing and running. Two boys,* **Kevin** *and* **Jimmy**, *are near* **Mrs Kay**]

Jimmy: 'Ey, miss, we could have brought our costumes an' gone swimmin'.

Kevin: We could go swimmin' anyway, couldn't we, miss?

Carol: [*Trailing behind* **Mrs Kay**] Miss, when do we have to go home?

Jimmy: What? In your undies?

Kevin: Yeh. Why not?

Mrs Kay: No. Not today.

Kevin: Agh . . . why not, miss.

Mrs Kay: Because. . . .

Jimmy: If y' went swimmin in just y' undies, the police would pick y' up, wouldn't they, miss?

Mrs Kay: Look, the reason I don't want you to go swimming is because there aren't enough staff here to guarantee that it would be safe. I want to go home with a full coachload thank you.

Carol: Miss, when d' we have t' go. . . .

Kevin: Agh, miss, I'd be all right, miss . . . I wouldn't get drowned, miss.

Mrs Kay: [*Warning*] Kevin!

Kevin: Oh, miss.

Mrs Kay: Kevin, I've already explained why I don't want you to go swimming. . . .

Kevin: Oh . . . Miss. . . .

Mrs Kay: Carry on like that and I'll have to sort you out.

Kevin: Agh. . . .

[*She stops him with a warning look. He tuts. Satisfied that he won't take it any further, she turns to* **Carol**]

Mrs Kay: Right. . . .

Kevin: Just for five minutes, miss.

Mrs Kay: [*Turning and walking towards him*] Kevin Bryant . . . come here.

Kevin: [*Backing away. Laughing*] Ah, miss, I didn't mean it . . . honest miss. I never meant it.

[**Mrs Kay**, *glaring in mock seriousness, comes after him. He is laughing. He breaks and runs. She chases him, skirts trailing in the water, with the other kids shouting and jeering and urging her to catch him.* **Kevin** *is hardly able to run because of laughing so much.* **Mrs Kay** *charges on through the water, looking incongruous.* **Kevin** *suddenly stops, turns, bends down in the water and prepares to send up a spray*]

Kevin: Don't, miss . . . don't or I'll spray y'.

Mrs Kay: Kevin Bryant . . . you'll do what? . . . You wait till I get hold of you.

[*They face each other. The* **Kids** *at the water's edge chant and shout: 'Get him, Miss', 'Duck him, Miss', 'Throw him in', 'Y've had it now, Bryant'.* **Kevin** *makes the mistake of turning to the group of* **Kids** *to answer them. In a flash she is on him and*

turns him upside down. She ducks him and he comes up splut-
tering and laughing. The other **Kids** *cheer and laugh*]

Kevin: Oh no, miss.

Mrs Kay: Now who wanted to go swimming, Kevin?

Kevin: Oh miss, miss. Me 'air's all wet.

[*She quickly lifts him so that she is carrying him, cradle fashion,*
out of the water. **Briggs** *looks on. He turns away.* **Mrs Kay** *and*
Kevin *walk away from the water. He shakes water from his*
hair]

Kevin: Miss . . . I might get a cold though. I hate that.

Mrs Kay: Oh, you're like an old woman. Come on then.

[*She reaches in her bag and produces a towel. She wraps the*
towel round his head and rubs vigorously. Beneath the towel
Kevin *is beaming and happy*]

Kevin: Ta miss.

Carol: [*At side of* **Mrs Kay**] Miss, when do we have t' go home?

Mrs Kay: What's the matter, love? Aren't you enjoying it?

Carol: Yeh, but I don't wanna go home. I wanna stay here.

Mrs Kay: Oh, Carol, love . . . we're here for at least another
hour. Why don't you start enjoying yourself instead of worry-
ing about going home.

Carol: Cos I don't wanna go home, miss.

Mrs Kay: Carol, love. . . . We have to go home. It can't be like
this all the time.

Carol: Why not?

Mrs Kay: [*Looks at her. Sighs*] I don't know, love.

Scene: **The rocks** [**Colin** *and* **Susan, Linda** *and* **Karen** *and some other kids are searching among the rocks.* **Reilly** *and* **Digga** *are nearby with a smaller group of followers. They are having a smoke behind a large rock*]

Andrews: Gis a drag.

Digga: Go an' buy some.

Andrews: Don't be sly, come on.

[**Reilly** *blows smoke in their faces. As they rush for it, he drops it and stubs it out in the sand with his foot. The* **Kids** *fight for it.* **Reilly** *turns away and looks out from the rock. He shouts across to* **Colin** *and* **Susan's** *group*]

Reilly: All right, miss.

[**Colin** *and* **Susan** *look up*]

Colin: [*Quietly*] Ah, here we go.

Reilly: [*Shouting over*] You comin' for a walk with me then, miss?

Colin: [*Standing and pointing. Shouting*] Look ... I'm warning you, Reilly.

Susan: Don't shout.

Colin: I'm just getting sick of him, that's all.

Susan: Well, why don't you go and have a word with him?

Colin: I don't know. I just can't seem to get through to friend Brian. For some reason he seems to have it in for me.

Susan: I wonder if I could get through to him.

Reilly: Come on ... what y' scared of?

Susan: You go back with the others.

Colin: What are you goin' to. . . .

Susan: Go on.

[**Colin** *moves off.* **Susan** *walks slowly across to* **Reilly**]

Linda: Has miss gone t' sort him out, sir?

Karen: He needs sortin' out, doesn't he, sir?

Linda: He's all right really, y' know, sir. Y' know, when he's on his own he's great.

Karen: Ooer . . . how d' you know?

Linda: Shut up you.

Colin: All right. All right.

[**Reilly** *smiles.* **Susan** *continues to walk slowly, provocatively, determinedly, towards him. As* **Susan** *stares straight at him,* **Reilly** *smiles bravely.* **Reilly's** *smile gradually disappears as she gets closer. She steps straight up to him – almost against him.* **Reilly** *looks anywhere but at her*]

Susan: [*Deliberately husky*] Well, Brian . . . I'm here.

Reilly: 'Ey, miss.

Susan: I'm all yours . . . handsome!

Reilly: Don't mess, miss.

Susan: [*Putting her arms around him*] I'm not messing, Big Boy. I'm serious.

[**Briggs**, *in the distance walking along the beach, stops and looks. He sees them then turns and goes back. Meanwhile,* **Reilly** *squirms*]

Susan: What's wrong?

Reilly: I was only havin' a laugh, miss.

[*Lots of little faces peer at them from around and on top of the surrounding rocks*]

Susan: You mean . . . don't tell me you weren't being serious, Brian.

Reilly: I was only jokin' with y', miss.

Susan: [*Keeping him pinned to the rock, quietly in his ear*] Well, you'd better listen to me Brian: [*Pause*] You're a hand-some lad, but I'd suggest that in future you stay in your own league instead of trying to take on ladies who could break you into little pieces. All right, we'll leave it at that shall we?

Reilly: Yes, miss.

[*She pats him gently on the face. She pulls back and as she begins to walk away the laughter breaks out.* **Reilly** *lunges out and the* **Kids** *scatter.* **Susan** *turns and sees this*]

Susan: Brian.

[*He looks up and she motions him over. She is now the teacher again*]

You know what we were saying about leagues?

Reilly: Yeh.

Susan: Well have you ever thought whose league Linda's in?

Reilly: [*Smiling*] Linda Croxley?

[**Susan** *nods.* **Reilly** *smiles*]

Agh 'ey miss, she doesn't fancy me. She's nuts about sir. No one else can get a chance.

Susan: I wouldn't be too sure about that.

[*Turns to go*]

See you.

Reilly: See y', miss.

[*He turns and walks back to his mates. As he appears they all start laughing and jeering. He stands smiling and proud*]

Reilly: Well! At least I'm not like you ugly gets. [*A pause during which he grows about two feet*] I . . . am handsome!

Scene: **The beach** [*A game of football is in progress.* **Mrs Kay** *is in goal. She makes a clumsy save and the* **Kids** *cheer.* **Briggs** *watches from a distance.* **Mrs Kay** *leaves the game and goes to meet* **Colin** *and* **Susan** *who are approaching*]

Mrs Kay: Wooh . . . I'm pooped.

Andrews: [*Shouting from game*] Agh, miss, we've not got a goaly now.

Mrs Kay: [*Shouting back*] It's all right, Carol can go in goal for you now.

[*She looks amongst the group.* **Colin** *and* **Susan** *look on*]

Where is she?

Susan: Who?

Mrs Kay: Carol. She went to look for you.

Colin: We haven't seen her.

Mrs Kay: Well, where is she?

[**Mrs Kay** *scans the beach.* **Carol** *cannot be seen.* **Mrs Kay** *looks at* **Susan**]

You haven't seen her at all?

[**Susan** *shakes her head*]

Mrs Kay: [*Looks over beach again*] Oh she couldn't. Could she?

Susan: Lost?

Mrs Kay: Don't say it. Perhaps he's seen her.

[*She shouts across*]

Mr Briggs . . . Mr Briggs.

[**Briggs** *looks up, rises and then comes over to her*]

Susan: I hope he has seen her.

Mrs Kay: Yeh. The only trouble is she didn't go that way.

Briggs: [*Approaching*] Is that it? Are we going home now?

Mrs Kay: Have you seen Carol Chandler in the last half hour?

Briggs: Look! I thought I'd made it quite plain that I was having nothing more to do with your outing.

Mrs Kay: Have you seen Carol Chandler?

Briggs: No. I haven't.

Mrs Kay: I think she might have wandered off somewhere.

Briggs: You mean you've lost her.

Mrs Kay: No. I mean she might have wandered off.

Briggs: Well, what's that if it's not losing her? All I can say is it's a wonder you haven't lost half a dozen of them.

Colin: Listen, Briggs, it's about time someone told you what a burke you are.

Briggs: And you listen, sonny. Don't you try telling me a word because you haven't even earned the right. Don't worry, when we get back to school, your number's up. As well as hers. [*He motions to* **Mrs Kay**] And you, [*To* **Susan**] I saw what was going on between you and Reilly. When we get back, I'll have the lot of you!

Mrs Kay: Would you mind postponing your threats until we've found Carol. At the moment I'd say the most important thing is to find the girl.

Briggs: Don't you mean *try* and find her?

Mrs Kay: Susan . . . you keep these lads playing football. We'll split up and look for her.

[**Mrs Kay**, **Colin** *and* **Briggs** *walk off in separate directions*]

Scene: **The cliff** [*Below the cliff-top, the sea is breaking on rocks in a cave mouth. In the distance,* **Mrs Kay** *is shouting 'Carol, Carol', and* **Colin** *is searching the far end of the beach.* **Carol** *is standing on top of the cliff watching the waves below. She looks out over the sea. Alone on the cliff-top, she is at peace with the warm sun and small breeze upon her – a fleeting moment of tranquility*]

Briggs: Carol Chandler!

[**Briggs** *approaches. On seeing her he stops and stands a few yards off*]

Just come here.

[*She turns and stares at him*]

Who gave you permission to come up here?

Carol: No one.

[*Turning, she dismisses him*]

Briggs: I'm talking to you, Carol Chandler.

[*She continues to ignore his presence*]

Now just listen here, young lady. . . .

[*As he goes to move towards her, she turns on him*]

Carol: Don't you come near me!

Briggs: [*Taken aback. Stopping*] Pardon!

Carol: I don't want you to come near me.

Briggs: Well, in that case just get yourself moving and let's get down to the beach.

[*Pause*]

Carol: You go. I'm not comin'.

Briggs: You what?

Carol: Tell Mrs Kay that she can go home without me. I'm stoppin' here . . . in Wales.

[*Pause*]

Briggs: Now just you listen to me — I've had just about enough today, just about enough, and I'm not putting up with a pile of silliness from the likes of you. Now come on. . . .

[*He starts to move towards her. She takes a step towards the edge of the cliff*]

Carol: Try an' get me an' I'll jump over.

[**Briggs** *stops, astounded. There is an angry pause. She continues to ignore him*]

Briggs: Now come on! I'll not tell you again.

[*He moves forward. Again, she moves nearer to the edge. He stops and they look at each other*]

I'll give you five seconds. Just five seconds. One . . . two . . . three . . . four . . . I'm warning you, five!

[*She stares at him blankly.* **Briggs** *stares back in impotent rage*]

Carol: I've told y' . . . I'm not comin' down with y'.

[*Pause*]

I'll jump y' know . . . I will.

Briggs: Just what are you trying to do to me?

Carol: I've told you. Leave me alone and I won't jump.

[*Pause*]

I wanna stay here. Where it's nice.

Briggs: Stay here? How could you stay here? What would you do? Where would you live?

Carol: I'd be all right.

Briggs: Now I've told you . . . stop being so silly.

Carol: [*Turning on him*] What do you worry for, eh? Eh? You don't care, do y'? Do y'?

Briggs: What? About you? Listen . . . if I didn't care, why am I here, now, trying to stop you doing something stupid.

Carol: Because if I jumped over, you'll get into trouble when you get back to school. That's why, Briggsy! So stop goin' on. You hate me.

Briggs: Don't be ridiculous — just because I'm a school teacher it doesn't mean to say that. . . .

Carol: Don't lie, you! I know you hate me. I've seen you goin' home in your car, passin' us on the street. And the way y' look at us. You hate all the kids.

[*She turns again to the sea, dismissing him*]

Briggs: What . . . makes you think that? Eh?

Carol: Why can't I just stay out here, eh? Why can't I live in one of them nice white houses an' do the garden an' that?

Briggs: Look . . . Carol . . . you're talking as though you've given up on life already. You sound as though life for you is just ending, instead of beginning. Now why can't, I mean, if it's what you want, what's to stop you working hard at school from now on, getting a good job and then moving out here when you're old enough? Eh?

Carol: [*Turns slowly to look at him. Contempt*] Don't be friggin' stupid.

[*She turns and looks down at the sea below*]

It's been a great day today. I loved it. I don't wanna leave here an' go home.

[*She moves to the edge of the cliff.* **Briggs** *is alarmed but unable to move*]

If I stayed though, it wouldn't be no good. You'd send the coppers to get me.

Briggs: We'd have to. How would you survive out here?

Carol: I know.

[*Pause*]

I'm not goin' back though.

Briggs: Please. . . .

Carol: Sir, sir, y' know if you'd been my old feller, I woulda been all right, wouldn't I?

[**Briggs** *slowly holds out his hand. She moves to the very edge of the cliff.* **Briggs** *is aware of how close she is*]

Briggs: Carol. Carol, please come away from there. [*Stretching out his hand to her*] Please.

[**Carol** *looks at him and a smile breaks across her face*]

Carol: Sir . . . sir you don't half look funny, y' know.

Briggs: [*Smiling back at her*] Why?

Carol: Sir, you should smile more often, y' look great when y' smile.

Briggs: Come on, Carol. [*He gingerly approaches her*]

Carol: What'll happen to me for doin' this, sir?

Briggs: Nothing. I promise you.

Carol: Sir, y' promisin' now, but what about when we get back t' school?

Briggs: [*Almost next to her now*] It won't be even mentioned.

[*She turns and looks down at the drop then back at* **Briggs's** *outstretched arm.* **Carol** *lifts her hand to his. She slips.* **Briggs** *grabs out quickly and manages to pull her to him.* **Briggs** *wraps his arms around her*]

Scene: **The beach** [**Susan** *still waits anxiously on the beach whilst the* **Kids** *play football. Other* **Kids** *watch the game, including* **Linda** *and* **Karen**. **Reilly** *challenges* **Digga** *for the ball and gets it from him*]

Karen: [*Shouting*] Go on, Digga . . . get him, get him.

Linda: Come on, Brian.

[**Reilly** *gets the ball past* **Digga**, *then around two more defenders, and scores.* **Linda** *cheers;* **Reilly** *sees her and winks.* **Mrs Kay** *and* **Colin** *approach.* **Susan** *looks up in inquiry;* **Mrs Kay** *shakes her head.* **Susan** *sighs*]

Mrs Kay: [*As she approaches*] I think we'd better let the police know.

Susan: Shall I keep them playing. . . .

[*Behind* **Mrs Kay**, **Susan** *can see* **Briggs** *and* **Carol** *in the distance*]

Oh, look . . . he's found her.

Mrs Kay: Oh, thank God. [*She turns and starts hurrying towards them*]

Colin: I'll bet he makes a bloody meal of this.

Susan: I don't care as long as she's safe.

Colin: Yeh, well, we'd better round them up. It'll be straight off now.

[**Mrs Kay** *approaches* **Carol** *and* **Briggs**]

Mrs Kay: Is she all right? Carol, the worry you've caused us!

Briggs: It's all right, Mrs Kay. I've dealt with all that.

Mrs Kay: Where were you?

Carol: On the cliff, miss.

Mrs Kay: On the. . . .

Briggs: Mrs Kay, I've found her. Now will you just let me deal with this.

Mrs Kay: [*Shaking her head as they walk up the beach towards the others*] Carol Chandler.

Briggs: Right.

[*The main group are preparing to leave as* **Mrs Kay**, **Carol** *and* **Briggs** *reach them*]

Briggs: Right . . . come on. Everyone on the coach.

[*General 'tuts' and moans of: 'Why can't we stay', etc.*]

Come on . . . all of you, on.

Scene: **The coach**   [*The staff stand by the coach doors as the* **Kids** *file by onto the coach*]

Driver: Right. [*To* **Briggs**] Back to the school then?

Briggs: School . . . back to school?

[**Mrs Kay** *looks up*]

It's only early, isn't it?

[*To* **Mrs Kay**] Anyway, you can't come all the way to the sea-side and not pay a visit to the fair.

[**Carol** *overhears them as she climbs onto the coach. She rushes inside*]

Carol: [*Loud whisper*] We're goin' the fair, we're goin' the fair. . . .. Sir's takin' us t' the fair.

[*The word is spread like fire inside the coach. Outside,* **Mrs Kay** *is intrigued – half-smiling*]

Briggs: Play your cards right, I might take even you for a ride on the waltzer.

Scene: **A fairground** [*Rock and roll music. On the waltzer the* **Kids**, *including* **Briggs** *and* **Carol** *together in a car, are spinning round.* **Mrs Kay** *takes a photograph of* **Briggs** *and* **Carol** *climbing out of the waltzer car.* **Mrs Kay**, **Colin** *and* **Susan**, **Reilly** *and* **Linda**, **Digga** *and* **Karen**, **Andrews**, **Ronson**, **Carol** *and some of the other kids are all photographed in a group.* **Briggs** *is snapped eating candy-floss, then again on the highest point of the bigwheel with mock fear on his face and* **Carol** *next to him her eyes closed in happy terror. Then he is photographed playing darts, then with a cowboy hat on handing a goldfish in a plastic bag to* **Carol**]

Scene: **Back at the coach** [*As the* **Kids** *pile onto the coach,* **Briggs**, *still wearing his cowboy hat, stands by the coach door*]

Kids: [*As they get onto coach*]
Sir, thanks, sir.
Sir, that was Ace.
We had a great laugh, didn't we, sir?
Sir, we gonna come here again?

Ronson: Can we come tomorrow, sir?

Briggs: Oh, get on the bus, Ronson.

[*Everyone is singing as the coach moves along. One of the kids is collecting for the* **Driver**; **Reilly** *has his arm around* **Linda**; **Digga** *is with* **Karen**; **Carol**, *with her goldfish, sits next to* **Mrs Kay**; **Ronson** *has a white mouse; the back seat is now occupied by* **Andrews** *and other kids.* **Briggs** *is also on the back seat — cowboy hat on, tie pulled down and singing with them.* **Mrs Kay** *takes a photograph of them*]

Mrs Kay: Say 'Cheese'.

Scene: **Back in the city**   [*The city can be seen out of the coach windows. Inside the coach the kids are tired and worn out now. Some are sleeping, some are singing softly to themselves, some stare blankly out of the window*]

Linda: Y' glad y' came?

Reilly: Yeh.

Linda: It was great wasn't it, eh?

Reilly: It'll be the last one I go on.

Linda: Why?

Reilly: Well I'm leaving in the summer aren't I?

Linda: What y' gonna do?

Reilly: [*Looking out of window*] Dunno.

[*Looks out of the window at the City*] It's friggin' horrible when y' come back to it, isn't it?

Linda: What is?

Reilly: That. [*Nods at window*]

Linda: Oh, yeh. [*Resigned*]

[**Briggs**, *with* **Andrews** *asleep next to him, sees the familiar surroundings and the kids hanging about in the streets. He sits up, puts his tie back to normal, goes to straighten his hair and feels the cowboy hat. He takes it off and puts in on* **Andrews**. *He then takes out a comb and combs his hair; puts on his jacket and walks down the aisle to* **Mrs Kay**]

Briggs: Well, nearly home.

Mrs Kay: [*She is taking the completed film from her camera*] I've got some gems of you here. We'll have one of these up in the staff room when they're developed.

Briggs: Eh? One of me?

Mrs Kay: Don't worry . . . I'm not going to let you forget the day you enjoyed yourself.

Briggs: [*Half laughs. Watches her put the film into its box*] Look . . . why don't you give it to me to develop?

Mrs Kay: Would you?

Briggs: Well, it would save you having to pay for it. I could do it in the lab.

Mrs Kay: [*Handing it over*] I don't know, using school facilities for personal use.

[*He smiles at her and takes the film. He puts it in his pocket*]

Scene: **Outside school**   [*It is evening as the coach turns into the street outside the school and pulls up.* **Briggs** *gets out, then the* **Kids** *pour out shouting 'Tarars' and running up the street.* **Reilly** *and* **Linda** *get off the coach together*]

Briggs: Right! Come on, everyone out!

Reilly: 'Night, sir. Enjoyed yourself today, didn't y', sir?

Briggs: Pardon?

Reilly: I didn't know you was like that, sir. Y' know, all right
for a laugh an' that. See y' tommorer, sir.

Briggs: Eh – Linda.

[*She stops.* **Briggs** *turns*]

We'll, erm, we'll let the uniform go this time.

[*Pause*]

But Linda, don't let me catch you dressing like that in the
future, though.

[*She shrugs and walks off with* **Reilly**. *The other kids make
their way home.* **Mrs Kay** *gets off the coach*]

Mrs Kay: Nothing left behind. 'Night Ronny.

Susan: Good night.

[*The coach pulls away. The* **Driver** *toots good-bye and they
wave*]

Ooh! . . . That's that. I don't know about anyone else but I'm
off for a drink.

Colin: Oh, I'll second that.

Susan: Good idea.

Mrs Kay: [*To* **Briggs**] You coming with us?

Briggs: [*The school looming behind him*] Well, actually I've. . . .

Susan: Oh, come on. . . .

Briggs: No . . . I'd better not. Thanks anyway. I've, um, lots of
marking to do at home. Thanks all the same though.

Mrs Kay: Oh well, if we can't twist your arm.

[*Pause*]

Thanks for today.

[*She turns and goes to her car accompanied by* **Susan** *and*

Colin. *She pulls away and toots good-bye.* **Briggs** *moves to his own car, puts his hand in his pocket and produces car keys and the roll of film. He looks at the film and then up at the school. He pulls open the film and exposes it to the light, crumples it up and puts it into his pocket. He then gets into his car, pulls away and at the junction turns right.* **Carol**, *walking along the street with the goldfish in her grasp, looks up at the disappearing car*]

The End

Follow-up Activities

Love is a Many Splendoured Thing

Discussion

What does Mickey think of girls at the beginning of the play?

What does he learn during the play? Which events and conversations lead him to change his mind?

What does Dawn learn during the play?

Do you think Dawn and Mickey are typical of girls and boys of their age?

Do girls 'grow up' more quickly than boys do? In what ways?

How do boys and girls attract each other's attention?

How do older people that you know regard 'young love'?

How do people of your age regard 'love'?

Improvisation

A scene in which two boys and two girls are reluctant to co-operate on a class project (in science or drama, for example), when their teacher has insisted on such co-operation.

Scenes in which young people interview each other about their opinions of the opposite sex.

A scene in which a girl tries to persuade a boy to take her to a football match; or to a dance.

The conversation that might take place between Mickey and Dawn when they next meet, after the action of the play.

A scene between Mickey and Dawn, thirty years on, when they are married and have children of their own.

A youth club scene in which the girls complain that the boys will not attend dances. The boys reply.

Writing

The diary entries that Mickey or Dawn might have written after the events described in the play.

An account of your first dance or of an outing or evening you are reminded of by the events enacted in the play.

Conduct and write up your own project on 'young love'.

A short play based on your own view of 'young love'.

On the Face of It

Discussion

How does 'having a door opened' by Mr Lamb show in Derry's home life?

Why does Derry's mother react as she does?

Apart from having lost a leg, how is Mr Lamb 'different' from many people?

What has Derry learned from Mr Lamb?

What effect do you think Mr Lamb's death will have on Derry?

What problems have you encountered when dealing with people who are handicapped or disturbed in some way? (For example, people who are in hospital or very upset emotionally, or people who are very shy or gloomy for some reason?)

Why are people afraid of deformity in others?

Improvisation

A scene in which Derry tells his mother about the death of Mr Lamb.

Conversations between Derry and people in his class at school (*a*) some time before this play begins and (*b*) after the events covered by the play.

A scene between yourself and a friend who has been severely injured in an accident and will be bed-ridden for some months or permanently handicapped or disfigured.

A conversation between an old person and a desperately shy young person, in which the older person gives the younger person the confidence to 'want the world'.

Writing

An account of a time when (like Derry) you have felt 'isolated' from others — perhaps when you were ill, when you were the only young person at an adult gathering, or when you had quar-relled with your friends.

A meeting between yourself and an adult who gave you courage and enthusiasm to do something you previously didn't dare to tackle.

A story or a short play in which a young person gains confi-dence from a conversation with an older person or an eccentric.

Mr Bruin Who Once Drove the Bus

Discussion

What memories of getting to school does this play awake? And what strange or comic incidents (either at your present school or at one you used to attend) does it remind you of?

Which characters in the play do you particularly 'recognize'? Why?

Would you say that Mr Bruin was irresponsible? What does the Headmaster think of him?

Discuss what adaptations you would have to make to the play before presenting it on stage. For example, who are the extra characters you would have to cast (such as Miss Jones)? Plan the mimes that might illustrate the narrator's descriptions (e.g. of what happens at the supermarket and on journeys to school, etc.).

Improvisation

Suppose Mrs Cupboard visited the Headmaster, instead of writing to him. Improvise the conversations they might have had.

A scene in which the Director of Education and Councillor Garbage meet the Headmaster to discuss Mr Bruin.

An interview between the Headmaster and Mr Bruin after the supermarket incident. Further scenes in which all those involved (the pupils, shoppers, and Mr Pilchard) report what happened.

An official investigation into the case of Mr Bruin, in which all the various characters defend Mr Bruin's behaviour or make their case against him. A jury could decide whether he was or was not 'irresponsible'. (This 'investigation' could take the form of a Parent-Teachers Association meeting.)

Writing

A dramatization of the events at the supermarket.

The letters the Director of Education might have written to the Headmaster, complaining about Mr Bruin's bad time-keeping and about his speeding.

Accounts of true events you have been reminded of by this play.

A story about an adult you know who is disapproved of by other adults because he or she is eccentric or irresponsible.

Your own play about the further adventures of Mr Bruin — perhaps when he has a job as a 'lollipop man' or a park attendant, or in a shop (such as a fish-and-chip shop).

Our Day Out

Discussion

Do the kids dislike Briggs? Are they afraid of him? Do they resent his strictness? Do all of them?

Do you think he is too strict? If so, when? Is he ever justified?

Why does he behave as he does at the fairground?

How do you think he will behave the next day at school?

Why does Mrs Kay behave as she does?

Do you think she is ever too easy-going? If so, when? Is she 'good' for the kids?

Do you think she is right just to want to give them a good day out?

What do you think of the various kids? Are they justified in their behaviour?

Do they deserve freedom and trust? If you were one of their teachers, how would you treat them?

How do the teachers in the play compare with ones you have known in the past?

In which parts (if anywhere) do you think this is an exaggerated picture of such a day out?

Improvisation

Scenes which might take place at school the next day — especially conversations between Briggs and the Headmaster, Mrs Kay and the Headmaster, Mrs Kay and Briggs, Briggs and Carol, Briggs and a group of the older kids, and between the kids who went on the outing and those who didn't.

The staffroom meeting that might be held to discuss the outing.

Scenes from a school outing you have been on.

The whole class could combine to make its own play about a school outing. Before beginning, plan carefully the roles each person will play and decide on the 'places' to be visited. Besides including scenes at these places, include the conversations that would take place before the outing, while travelling and (perhaps) on returning.

Create a 'documentary' play discussing the behaviour of young people today, in which television reporters 'film' and interview the adults and young people we see in the film. (This could be presented on stage or recorded on tape.)

Writing

Write up some of your improvisations into a play or filmscript about the day at school after *Our Day Out*.

Write a short story, play or filmscript about a school trip you have been on.